Sustainable Finance for Ecosystem Restoration: Unlocking Investment for Environmental Solutions

Copyright

Sustainable Finance for Ecosystem Restoration: Unlocking Investment for Environmental Solutions

© 2025 Robert C. Brears

Published by **Global Climate Solutions**

ISBNs:

Ebook: 978-1-991369-05-5

Paperback: 978-1-991369-06-2

Table of Contents

Preface

The global environmental crisis is accelerating at an unprecedented pace. Ecosystems are being degraded, biodiversity is declining, and climate change is intensifying, placing immense pressure on natural resources and communities worldwide. While scientific advancements and policy commitments have made progress in addressing these challenges, one fundamental barrier remains: financing. Without sufficient and sustained investment, large-scale ecosystem restoration efforts cannot reach the scale required to make a lasting impact.

Sustainable Finance for Ecosystem Restoration: Unlocking Investment for Environmental Solutions is a response to this critical need. It explores how financial mechanisms, innovative investment models, and policy frameworks can mobilize the capital necessary to restore landscapes, protect biodiversity, and build climate resilience. The financial sector, corporations, governments, and civil society all have a role to play in closing the restoration funding gap, ensuring that economic development aligns with environmental sustainability.

This book is designed to provide a clear roadmap for decision-makers, investors, and sustainability professionals seeking to integrate restoration finance into their strategies. It highlights emerging opportunities in market-based solutions such as carbon and biodiversity credits, green bonds, and impact investing while emphasizing the importance of strong governance, risk management, and multi-stakeholder collaboration.

The urgency to act has never been greater. With nature-based solutions gaining recognition as an essential tool for achieving climate and sustainability goals, the time has come to harness the power of finance to drive ecosystem restoration at scale. By bridging the gap between economic imperatives and environmental needs, we can unlock investment for a more resilient and sustainable future.

Introduction

Ecosystem restoration is essential for reversing environmental degradation, enhancing biodiversity, and improving climate resilience. However, large-scale restoration efforts require significant financial resources, which are often limited or inadequately allocated. Traditional funding sources, such as government grants and international aid, are insufficient to meet the growing demand for restoration initiatives. Sustainable finance has emerged as a critical solution, leveraging public and private sector investments to support long-term ecological recovery.

Sustainable finance integrates environmental, social, and governance (ESG) principles into investment decisions, ensuring that financial flows contribute to ecological and economic sustainability. This approach includes diverse financial instruments, such as green bonds, carbon credits, and impact investments, which incentivize restoration while generating financial returns. As global environmental challenges intensify, sustainable finance provides a scalable framework for mobilizing resources, aligning economic incentives with environmental stewardship, and promoting resilience in ecosystems that sustain human and planetary well-being.

The Need for Financial Mechanisms to Scale Restoration

Despite growing recognition of ecosystem restoration's importance, financial barriers continue to limit its large-scale implementation. The cost of restoring degraded landscapes, rehabilitating watersheds, and reviving biodiversity-rich ecosystems often exceeds the available funding from traditional sources. Many restoration projects lack access to long-term, stable financial mechanisms, making them vulnerable to budget fluctuations and policy shifts.

To address these challenges, innovative financial mechanisms are required to attract investments from diverse stakeholders, including governments, corporations, philanthropic organizations, and private investors. Mechanisms such as blended finance, payments for ecosystem services (PES), and sustainability-linked loans help de-risk investments, making restoration projects more attractive to capital markets. Additionally, integrating restoration finance with climate adaptation and resilience strategies enhances financial viability by aligning restoration with broader economic and social benefits. By developing scalable, transparent, and results-driven financial mechanisms, restoration efforts can expand, creating lasting ecological and economic value.

Key Financial Instruments, Investment Trends, and Policies

Sustainable finance for ecosystem restoration relies on a combination of investment tools, market-based mechanisms, and policy frameworks. Green bonds, impact investments, and conservation finance mechanisms provide structured funding sources for large-scale restoration initiatives. Carbon markets and biodiversity credits create economic incentives for ecosystem protection and rehabilitation. Meanwhile, regulatory frameworks and government policies play a crucial role in ensuring financial accountability, risk management, and long-term project viability.

Recent trends indicate a growing shift toward nature-based investments, as financial institutions and corporations recognize the economic value of healthy ecosystems. Aligning finance with environmental objectives strengthens global sustainability efforts, bridging the gap between ecological conservation and economic growth.

Structure of the Book

This book explores the role of sustainable finance in unlocking investment for ecosystem restoration. It examines key financial mechanisms, public and private sector contributions, and policy frameworks that support large-scale restoration efforts. Each chapter delves into specific financial instruments, including green bonds, impact investments, and market-based solutions.

Additionally, the book highlights challenges and opportunities in financing restoration, emphasizing governance, risk management, and innovation. By providing a comprehensive analysis of sustainable finance for ecosystem restoration, this book serves as a guide for policymakers, investors, and environmental practitioners seeking to scale up restoration efforts through effective financial strategies.

Chapter 1: The Need for Sustainable Finance in Ecosystem Restoration

Ecosystem restoration plays a critical role in reversing environmental degradation, enhancing biodiversity, and strengthening climate resilience. However, achieving large-scale restoration requires significant financial resources that are often insufficient or inconsistently allocated. Traditional funding models, such as government grants and international aid, have proven inadequate to meet the rising demand for restoration projects. As global commitments to environmental sustainability grow, there is an increasing need for innovative financial solutions that can mobilize investments at scale.

Sustainable finance provides a structured approach to funding restoration efforts by integrating ESG considerations into investment decisions. By leveraging both public and private capital, sustainable finance enables long-term, stable funding mechanisms that support large-scale ecological recovery. This chapter examines the financial challenges associated with ecosystem restoration, explores the role of different funding sources, and highlights the urgent need for financial innovation to bridge existing investment gaps.

Defining Ecosystem Restoration and Its Global Importance

Ecosystem restoration refers to the process of assisting the recovery of degraded, damaged, or destroyed ecosystems to improve their ecological functionality, biodiversity, and long-term resilience. This practice encompasses a wide range of interventions, from reforestation and wetland rehabilitation to soil regeneration and marine habitat restoration. The goal of restoration is not only to repair ecosystems but also to enhance their ability to provide essential services such as clean water, carbon sequestration, soil fertility, and climate regulation. Healthy ecosystems contribute to food security, economic stability, and overall human well-being, making restoration a crucial environmental and socio-economic strategy.

The Role of Ecosystem Services

Ecosystem services are the benefits that natural systems provide to people and the planet. They are generally classified into four categories: provisioning, regulating, cultural, and supporting services. Provisioning services include food, fresh water, timber, and medicinal resources, while regulating services encompass climate regulation, flood control, and disease prevention. Cultural services provide recreational, aesthetic, and spiritual value, and supporting services, such as nutrient cycling and soil formation, maintain the conditions necessary for life.

Degraded ecosystems result in the loss of these critical services, leading to increased vulnerability to natural disasters, declining agricultural productivity, and greater exposure to climate change impacts. Ecosystem restoration, therefore, serves as a means to reverse these negative effects by restoring ecological balance and strengthening resilience against environmental shocks.

The Global Importance of Ecosystem Restoration

Ecosystem restoration has gained increasing international recognition as a key strategy for addressing environmental and climate challenges. The United Nations declared 2021–2030 as the Decade on Ecosystem Restoration, emphasizing the need for urgent global action to restore landscapes, water bodies, and natural habitats. This initiative aligns with global commitments such as the Paris Agreement on climate change, the Convention on Biological Diversity (CBD), and the Sustainable Development Goals (SDGs), particularly Goal 15, which focuses on life on land, and Goal 14, which addresses life below water.

Restoration efforts support biodiversity conservation by providing habitats for endangered species and fostering ecological connectivity between fragmented landscapes. In many regions, deforestation, soil erosion, and habitat destruction have led to species decline, but targeted restoration efforts can help reverse these trends. For example, reforestation and afforestation programs not only increase forest cover but also contribute to carbon sequestration, mitigating climate change while restoring biodiversity.

Economic and Social Benefits

Beyond ecological gains, ecosystem restoration delivers significant economic and social benefits. Restored landscapes enhance agricultural productivity by improving soil health and water availability, reducing the risks of desertification and land degradation. Wetland and mangrove restoration projects contribute to coastal protection, preventing property damage from storms and flooding while supporting fisheries and tourism industries.

Restoration also generates employment opportunities in fields such as forestry, sustainable agriculture, and conservation management. The transition to nature-based solutions creates green jobs and fosters sustainable economic growth. Additionally, communities that rely on healthy ecosystems for their livelihoods, such as indigenous groups and rural populations, benefit directly from restoration efforts that enhance natural resource availability and environmental stability.

Challenges and the Need for Sustainable Finance

Despite the clear benefits of ecosystem restoration, financing remains a major barrier to large-scale implementation. Restoration projects require long-term investments, and many initiatives struggle with financial uncertainty, limited public funding, and insufficient private sector engagement. Sustainable finance plays a crucial role in addressing these gaps by leveraging public and private capital to support restoration projects.

As global recognition of restoration's importance continues to grow, financial mechanisms must evolve to facilitate large-scale, long-term investment in ecosystem recovery. Innovative financing strategies, such as green bonds, impact investing, and payment for ecosystem services, can help bridge the funding gap and ensure that restoration efforts are not only initiated but sustained over time.

Financial Gaps and Challenges in Restoration Investments

Ecosystem restoration is a critical global priority, yet securing sufficient and sustained funding remains one of its greatest challenges. Despite increasing recognition of the ecological, economic, and social benefits of restoration, financial barriers continue to hinder large-scale implementation. Many restoration projects struggle to attract investment due to high upfront costs, uncertain returns, and long payback periods. Addressing these financial gaps is essential to ensuring that ecosystem restoration efforts can be effectively scaled and sustained over time.

Insufficient Public Funding and Budget Constraints

Governments play a significant role in financing restoration projects through public funding, grants, and subsidies. However, national and local budgets are often constrained by competing priorities such as infrastructure development, healthcare, and education. As a result, environmental initiatives, including restoration efforts, frequently receive inadequate financial support. Many governments lack the financial resources to commit to large-scale, long-term restoration programs, leaving a significant funding gap that limits progress.

Additionally, public sector funding is often fragmented and inconsistent, leading to challenges in maintaining restoration projects beyond their initial implementation. Without stable and predictable financial support, many projects struggle to achieve their intended ecological and socio-economic benefits.

11

Limited Private Sector Engagement

Private sector investment in ecosystem restoration remains relatively low compared to other sustainability initiatives, such as renewable energy and energy efficiency. One of the key reasons for this is the perception that restoration projects lack direct financial returns or immediate profitability. Many businesses and investors prioritize projects with clear revenue generation models, while restoration efforts often deliver long-term benefits that are not immediately monetizable.

Another challenge is the lack of standardized financial frameworks and risk assessment tools for ecosystem restoration investments. Unlike traditional infrastructure projects, restoration initiatives do not always have clear metrics for measuring financial returns, making them less attractive to investors. This uncertainty deters private sector participation and limits the availability of commercial financing for restoration.

High Upfront Costs and Long Payback Periods

Restoration projects often require significant initial investments in activities such as land acquisition, reforestation, habitat reconstruction, and biodiversity conservation. These costs can be prohibitive for many organizations, particularly in developing countries where financial resources are scarce. Furthermore, the benefits of restoration, such as improved ecosystem services, carbon sequestration, and enhanced biodiversity, may take years or even decades to materialize.

The long payback period associated with restoration investments poses a major challenge for investors seeking short- or medium-term financial returns. Unlike traditional infrastructure projects that generate immediate revenue through user fees or energy production, ecosystem restoration projects typically rely on indirect benefits, such as improved water quality, soil health, or climate resilience, which are difficult to monetize.

Lack of Financial Mechanisms and Incentives

Existing financial mechanisms for ecosystem restoration are often inadequate, fragmented, or difficult to access. While some funding sources, such as grants, philanthropic donations, and government subsidies, are available, they are often short-term and project-specific. There is a need for more scalable financial mechanisms that can provide long-term funding for restoration efforts.

Innovative financial instruments, such as green bonds, biodiversity credits, and PES, have the potential to bridge this gap. However, many of these mechanisms are still in their early stages of development and require greater market adoption. Additionally, regulatory and policy frameworks must evolve to provide stronger incentives for private investment in restoration.

Moving Toward Scalable Financial Solutions

Addressing the financial challenges of ecosystem restoration requires a multi-faceted approach that combines public and private investment, innovative financing mechanisms, and supportive policy frameworks. Governments, businesses, financial institutions, and conservation organizations must collaborate to develop scalable financial solutions that reduce investment risks and create new revenue streams for restoration projects.

By overcoming these financial barriers, restoration efforts can be expanded and sustained, ensuring that ecosystems continue to provide essential services for future generations.

Public vs. Private Funding Roles in Restoration

Ecosystem restoration requires substantial financial resources, and both public and private sectors play essential roles in funding these initiatives. While governments have traditionally been the primary source of funding for restoration, the scale of environmental degradation has created a growing need for private sector investment. Each sector brings unique strengths and challenges to restoration financing, and leveraging their complementary roles is critical for scaling up global restoration efforts.

Public Sector Funding: Government Investments and Policy Support

Governments provide significant financial resources for restoration through national budgets, grants, subsidies, and international aid. Public sector funding is crucial for large-scale restoration projects that require long-term investments, such as reforestation, wetland rehabilitation, and soil restoration. Governments also play a regulatory role, setting environmental policies and frameworks that guide restoration activities and encourage sustainable land management practices.

Public funding often comes in the form of direct investments, where governments allocate resources for restoration through agencies, conservation programs, or public works projects. Many governments also establish incentive programs, such as tax credits or subsidies, to encourage private landowners and businesses to participate in restoration efforts. Additionally, international organizations and multilateral development banks provide funding to support ecosystem restoration in developing countries.

Despite these contributions, public sector funding alone is insufficient to meet global restoration needs. Budget constraints, competing priorities, and political changes can limit the availability and consistency of government funding. As a result, public financing must be complemented by private sector investment to close the funding gap.

Private Sector Investment: Unlocking Market-Driven Solutions

The private sector plays a crucial role in ecosystem restoration by mobilizing capital through impact investing, sustainability-linked bonds, and market-based mechanisms such as carbon credits and biodiversity offsets. Unlike public funding, which is often dependent on government budgets and policy decisions, private investment can provide more flexible and scalable financial solutions.

Corporations are increasingly recognizing the economic and reputational benefits of investing in ecosystem restoration. Many companies integrate restoration projects into their corporate sustainability strategies, particularly those operating in industries reliant on natural resources, such as agriculture, forestry, and water management. Businesses also participate in restoration through corporate social responsibility (CSR) initiatives and voluntary carbon offset programs.

Institutional investors, such as pension funds and asset managers, are also becoming more involved in restoration finance through impact investment funds that seek both financial returns and positive environmental outcomes. Additionally, private philanthropy plays a role in funding restoration, with foundations and high-net-worth individuals contributing to conservation projects through donations and endowments.

Challenges in Public-Private Collaboration

While both public and private sectors contribute to restoration finance, challenges remain in aligning their efforts effectively. Public sector funding is often slow-moving and bureaucratic, while private sector investments require clear financial incentives and risk mitigation strategies. The lack of standardized frameworks for measuring the financial returns of restoration projects can also deter private investors.

Public-private partnerships (PPPs) offer a solution by combining government funding with private sector expertise and resources. PPPs can help reduce financial risks, create shared accountability, and improve the long-term viability of restoration projects. However, these partnerships require strong governance structures, clear regulations, and transparent funding mechanisms to ensure success.

The Need for an Integrated Funding Approach

To scale up ecosystem restoration, a blended financing approach is necessary—one that leverages both public funding for foundational support and private investment for market-driven solutions. Governments can create enabling environments for private sector participation through regulatory incentives, risk-sharing mechanisms, and co-financing arrangements. At the same time, businesses and investors must recognize the long-term value of healthy ecosystems and integrate restoration into their financial strategies.

By strengthening collaboration between public and private funding sources, ecosystem restoration efforts can be expanded, ensuring that degraded landscapes and ecosystems are restored for future generations.

Global Restoration Targets and Financial Needs

Ecosystem restoration has become a global priority, reflected in various international agreements and initiatives that set ambitious targets for reversing environmental degradation. The United Nations Decade on Ecosystem Restoration (2021–2030) serves as a major global effort to accelerate restoration activities and integrate them into broader environmental and development goals. This initiative aligns with the SDGs, particularly SDG 15 (Life on Land) and SDG 14 (Life Below Water), which emphasize the protection and restoration of terrestrial and marine ecosystems.

In addition to the UN Decade, the Bonn Challenge aims to restore 350 million hectares of degraded and deforested land by 2030. Launched in 2011 by the International Union for Conservation of Nature (IUCN) and the German government, the initiative has gained commitments from over 60 countries. Similarly, the AFR100 (African Forest Landscape Restoration Initiative) seeks to restore 100 million hectares in Africa by 2030, while the Initiative 20x20 focuses on restoring 20 million hectares in Latin America.

Despite these commitments, the financial resources required to achieve global restoration targets remain insufficient. The estimated cost of restoring degraded ecosystems worldwide is in the range of hundreds of billions of dollars annually. The World Economic Forum estimates that transitioning to a nature-positive economy could generate $10 trillion in business value by 2030, yet current investments in ecosystem restoration fall far short of this potential.

Public funding alone cannot bridge the financial gap. While governments and international organizations contribute significant funding through grants, subsidies, and development aid, there is an urgent need for increased private sector investment. Financial mechanisms such as green bonds, biodiversity credits, and PES offer opportunities to mobilize additional capital. Impact investing, which seeks both financial returns and environmental benefits, is also gaining traction as a way to fund large-scale restoration projects.

To meet global restoration targets, financial strategies must be diversified, blending public, private, and philanthropic funding sources. Governments must create enabling policies that encourage investment, while businesses and financial institutions need to integrate restoration into their sustainability and risk management frameworks. By closing the financial gap, restoration efforts can be scaled up, ensuring that degraded ecosystems are restored to support biodiversity, climate resilience, and human well-being.

Conclusion

Sustainable finance plays a critical role in addressing the funding challenges associated with large-scale ecosystem restoration. While restoration efforts are increasingly recognized as essential for biodiversity conservation, climate resilience, and long-term resource sustainability, significant financial gaps remain. Without sufficient investment, many projects struggle to achieve their intended environmental and social outcomes. Mobilizing capital from both public and private sources is necessary to scale up restoration initiatives and integrate them into broader economic and policy frameworks.

Public funding and policy incentives provide a foundation for restoration finance, but they are not sufficient on their own. Private sector engagement is essential for expanding financial resources and ensuring long-term sustainability. Market-based mechanisms, such as carbon credits, biodiversity offsets, and sustainability-linked financial instruments, offer opportunities to align financial returns with ecological benefits. Encouraging businesses to incorporate restoration efforts into their sustainability strategies can further support investment in nature-based solutions.

Governments and financial institutions have a key role in creating conditions that support restoration finance. Establishing clear regulatory frameworks, developing transparent reporting mechanisms, and implementing risk-sharing models can help attract investment while ensuring accountability. Strengthening governance and multi-stakeholder collaboration will further enhance financial flows and improve project outcomes.

The increasing demand for sustainable finance presents an opportunity to integrate restoration into mainstream investment strategies. By aligning economic incentives with conservation priorities, financial mechanisms can be designed to close funding gaps and expand restoration efforts globally. As financial tools and policies continue to evolve, ensuring that restoration projects receive adequate investment will be essential for achieving long-term environmental and economic stability.

Chapter 2: Public Finance and Policy Incentives for Ecosystem Restoration

Public finance plays a fundamental role in supporting ecosystem restoration, providing essential funding, regulatory frameworks, and policy incentives that drive large-scale environmental recovery. Governments and international institutions allocate financial resources through grants, subsidies, tax incentives, and direct investments to promote restoration initiatives. However, given the scale of global environmental degradation, these funds alone are insufficient to meet long-term restoration goals.

Effective policy frameworks are essential for mobilizing financial resources and ensuring the sustainability of restoration efforts. Governments use legislation, fiscal incentives, and regulatory mechanisms to create enabling environments that attract investment in restoration. Additionally, international organizations, including the United Nations, the World Bank, and regional development banks, provide financial support and technical assistance to countries implementing restoration projects.

This chapter explores the various public finance mechanisms and policy incentives that drive ecosystem restoration. It examines government funding models, the role of international institutions, the impact of PPPs, and how national policies can strengthen financial commitments to restoration efforts. By understanding these financial and policy instruments, stakeholders can better align restoration initiatives with long-term sustainability goals.

Overview of Government Funding Models

Governments play a critical role in financing ecosystem restoration through a range of funding models designed to support environmental recovery, biodiversity conservation, and climate resilience. These funding mechanisms provide essential financial resources for large-scale restoration initiatives, particularly in cases where private sector investment remains limited. Effective government funding models ensure long-term sustainability, encourage stakeholder participation, and align restoration efforts with national and global environmental goals.

Direct Government Investments

One of the most common funding models involves direct government investments in restoration projects. Governments allocate funds through national budgets to support afforestation, wetland restoration, soil conservation, and other ecological initiatives. These investments are often implemented by environmental agencies, public-sector institutions, and local municipalities. Direct investments ensure that restoration projects receive stable funding and align with national conservation priorities.

However, budget constraints can limit the scale and consistency of government-funded restoration programs. Economic downturns and shifting political priorities may lead to reduced environmental expenditures, creating challenges in maintaining long-term restoration efforts. To address these limitations, governments often seek additional funding sources, including international financial assistance and partnerships with private sector stakeholders.

Grants and Subsidies

Grants and subsidies provide targeted financial support to organizations, businesses, and communities engaged in restoration activities. Many governments establish grant programs that offer funding for ecosystem restoration, reforestation, and sustainable land management. These programs enable non-governmental organizations (NGOs), research institutions, and community groups to implement localized restoration initiatives.

Subsidies, on the other hand, incentivize landowners and businesses to adopt sustainable land-use practices. For example, agricultural subsidies may encourage farmers to restore degraded land, implement soil conservation techniques, or maintain riparian buffer zones. By reducing financial barriers, grants and subsidies make restoration projects more accessible and economically viable.

Tax Incentives and Fiscal Policies

Governments use tax incentives as a financial tool to promote investment in ecosystem restoration. Tax credits, deductions, and exemptions encourage businesses and individuals to participate in environmental restoration projects. For example, landowners who restore wetlands or reforest degraded land may receive tax deductions for conservation expenditures. Similarly, businesses investing in sustainable land-use practices may benefit from reduced corporate tax rates.

In addition to tax incentives, fiscal policies such as environmental levies and pollution taxes generate revenue that can be reinvested in restoration efforts. Carbon pricing mechanisms, including carbon taxes and emissions trading systems, provide financial resources for reforestation and carbon sequestration projects. These policies create financial incentives for industries to mitigate environmental impacts while funding restoration programs.

International Financial Assistance

Many governments rely on international financial institutions and development agencies to fund large-scale restoration projects. Organizations such as the United Nations Development Programme (UNDP), the World Bank, and the Global Environment Facility (GEF) provide financial support for restoration initiatives, particularly in developing countries. These funds are often allocated through grants, concessional loans, and technical assistance programs.

Bilateral agreements between governments also facilitate cross-border restoration efforts. Countries with shared ecosystems, such as transboundary rivers or forests, may establish joint financing mechanisms to restore and conserve these critical habitats. International financial assistance strengthens global cooperation in restoration and supports countries with limited financial resources.

PPPs

PPPs offer an innovative approach to financing restoration by combining government funding with private sector investment. Through PPPs, governments collaborate with businesses, financial institutions, and non-profits to implement large-scale restoration projects. These partnerships leverage public funds to de-risk private investments, creating a more attractive financial environment for ecosystem restoration.

By utilizing diverse funding models, governments can enhance financial sustainability, expand restoration efforts, and ensure long-term ecosystem recovery. Strengthening these financial mechanisms is essential for meeting global restoration targets and addressing environmental challenges.

International Institutions' Role in Funding

International institutions play a vital role in financing ecosystem restoration by providing financial resources, technical assistance, and policy guidance to governments, NGOs, and private sector stakeholders. These institutions include multilateral development banks, global environmental funds, and United Nations agencies, all of which contribute to large-scale restoration efforts, particularly in developing countries where financial constraints often limit progress. Their support helps ensure that restoration projects align with global environmental commitments and contribute to long-term sustainability goals.

Multilateral Development Banks (MDBs)

MDBs, such as the World Bank, the Inter-American Development Bank (IDB), and the Asian Development Bank (ADB), provide significant financial assistance for ecosystem restoration. These banks offer concessional loans, grants, and technical support to governments and regional organizations undertaking restoration projects. MDBs also facilitate public-private partnerships by co-financing projects with private investors, reducing financial risks, and attracting additional capital.

The World Bank's PROGREEN program is an example of an initiative supporting landscape restoration and sustainable land use. Similarly, the ADB funds nature-based solutions to enhance climate resilience and biodiversity conservation. These institutions prioritize restoration projects that align with national development plans, ensuring that financial support contributes to broader economic and environmental goals.

Global Environmental Funds

Several global environmental funds provide targeted financial support for restoration. The GEF, established in 1991, is a key source of funding for biodiversity conservation, climate adaptation, and land restoration. The GEF finances projects that support sustainable land management, reforestation, and wetland rehabilitation, particularly in developing countries.

The Green Climate Fund (GCF) is another major funding mechanism focused on climate adaptation and mitigation. Many restoration projects qualify for GCF financing, especially those integrating carbon sequestration, watershed management, and ecosystem-based adaptation. The fund channels resources toward projects that align with the Paris Agreement and the United Nations SDGs.

Additionally, the Land Degradation Neutrality Fund (LDN Fund), managed by the United Nations Convention to Combat Desertification (UNCCD), mobilizes private investment to restore degraded land and promote sustainable agriculture. By blending public and private capital, these funds create opportunities for large-scale ecosystem restoration.

United Nations Agencies and International Organizations

Several United Nations agencies play a key role in funding and coordinating restoration efforts. The United Nations Environment Programme (UNEP) leads initiatives that support reforestation, biodiversity conservation, and sustainable land-use policies. UNEP also provides technical guidance and capacity-building programs to help countries implement restoration projects effectively.

The Food and Agriculture Organization (FAO) supports agroforestry, soil conservation, and sustainable agricultural practices that contribute to land restoration. FAO's initiatives help ensure that restoration efforts align with food security and rural development objectives.

The United Nations Development Programme (UNDP) provides financial and technical assistance for sustainable development projects, including nature-based solutions for climate adaptation and disaster risk reduction. UNDP works closely with national governments to integrate restoration into broader development strategies.

Regional and Bilateral Financial Mechanisms

In addition to multilateral institutions, regional organizations and bilateral financial mechanisms provide funding for restoration. The African Forest Landscape Restoration Initiative (AFR100) mobilizes financial resources to restore 100 million hectares of degraded land in Africa by 2030. Similarly, Initiative 20x20 focuses on restoring 20 million hectares in Latin America, with financial support from international donors and private investors.

Bilateral financial agreements between countries also support restoration. Governments in wealthier nations often provide funding to developing countries through environmental aid programs and sustainable development grants. These partnerships enhance cross-border cooperation in restoration and conservation efforts.

PPPs in Restoration

PPPs play an increasingly important role in financing and implementing ecosystem restoration projects. By combining public sector resources with private sector investment and expertise, PPPs provide a sustainable model for large-scale restoration efforts. Governments often lack sufficient funding and technical capacity to undertake ambitious restoration initiatives alone, while private companies may require financial incentives or risk-sharing mechanisms to participate. PPPs help bridge this gap by fostering collaboration and ensuring long-term project sustainability.

The Role of Governments in PPPs

Governments play a central role in establishing PPP frameworks for restoration. They provide initial funding, policy support, and regulatory structures to create an enabling environment for private investment. This includes offering financial incentives such as tax credits, subsidies, and grants to attract private sector participation. Additionally, governments ensure that PPP projects align with national and international restoration targets, ensuring compliance with environmental laws and sustainability commitments.

In many cases, governments allocate public land for restoration projects, allowing private investors to develop conservation and reforestation initiatives while maintaining public ownership. This model helps balance ecological restoration goals with economic interests, ensuring that projects deliver both environmental and financial benefits.

Private Sector Contributions to PPPs

The private sector brings financial investment, technical expertise, and innovation to PPPs. Businesses invest in restoration for various reasons, including regulatory compliance, CSR, and alignment with ESG principles. Many companies in industries such as forestry, agriculture, and water management view ecosystem restoration as a long-term investment that enhances their supply chain resilience and brand reputation.

Financial institutions, including banks and impact investors, also participate in PPPs by providing capital for restoration projects. By leveraging blended finance models, where public funds de-risk private investments, PPPs can attract institutional investors looking for sustainable investment opportunities.

Examples of PPP Financing Mechanisms

Several financial models support PPPs in restoration:

- **Co-Financing Agreements:** Governments and private companies jointly fund restoration projects, sharing both financial risks and benefits. These agreements often involve international donors and development banks that provide concessional loans or guarantees.
- **Payment for Ecosystem Services (PES):** Private entities, such as water utilities or agribusinesses, pay for restoration activities that enhance ecosystem services, such as improved water quality or carbon sequestration.
- **Green Bonds and Sustainability-Linked Bonds:** Public entities issue bonds to raise capital for restoration projects, with private investors purchasing these bonds as part of their sustainable investment portfolios.
- **Concession Agreements:** Governments grant private companies the rights to restore and manage degraded land or ecosystems under long-term contracts, ensuring financial viability through sustainable business models such as ecotourism or carbon credit trading.

Challenges in Implementing PPPs for Restoration

Despite their potential, PPPs in restoration face several challenges. One of the key issues is balancing financial profitability with ecological integrity. Private sector investors often seek clear financial returns, which may not align with the long-term benefits of ecosystem restoration. Ensuring that restoration projects generate sustainable revenue streams is essential for attracting private investment.

Regulatory and governance challenges also arise, as unclear policies or weak enforcement can undermine PPP effectiveness. Governments must establish transparent legal frameworks, clear accountability mechanisms, and performance monitoring systems to ensure that private sector partners fulfill their environmental commitments.

The Future of PPPs in Restoration

Expanding PPPs in restoration requires continued innovation in financing mechanisms, stronger regulatory frameworks, and increased collaboration between public institutions, private companies, and civil society organizations. By leveraging public and private resources effectively, PPPs can accelerate large-scale restoration efforts, ensuring ecological resilience and long-term sustainability.

National Policy Incentives for Financing Restoration

National governments play a crucial role in promoting ecosystem restoration through policy incentives that encourage investment and long-term financial support. By implementing targeted policies, governments can create favorable conditions for businesses, financial institutions, and landowners to engage in restoration activities. These incentives not only attract private capital but also ensure that restoration aligns with broader economic and environmental objectives.

Tax Incentives and Fiscal Benefits

Many governments use tax incentives to encourage restoration investments. Tax credits, deductions, and exemptions can reduce the financial burden on businesses and individuals engaging in restoration projects. For example, landowners who reforest degraded land or restore wetlands may qualify for tax deductions on conservation-related expenses. Similarly, businesses investing in sustainable land management or carbon sequestration projects may receive corporate tax benefits.

Governments also implement reduced property tax rates for landowners who dedicate portions of their land to conservation and restoration efforts. These fiscal incentives make long-term ecological restoration financially viable, particularly in areas where land degradation threatens economic productivity.

Subsidies and Direct Financial Support

Subsidy programs provide direct financial support to farmers, businesses, and community groups engaged in restoration activities. Governments allocate funds to cover a portion of the costs associated with afforestation, soil rehabilitation, and wetland restoration. These programs help reduce the financial risks associated with large-scale restoration, making projects more accessible to private investors and land managers.

Some countries also implement cost-sharing programs, where governments and private stakeholders jointly fund restoration initiatives. This collaborative approach ensures that public and private sectors share financial responsibility while achieving common restoration goals.

Regulatory Frameworks and Market-Based Incentives

Strong regulatory frameworks create an environment where restoration investment is both necessary and financially attractive.

Policies requiring businesses to mitigate environmental impacts through restoration projects, such as biodiversity offset programs, generate private sector demand for restoration investments.

Additionally, market-based mechanisms like PES and carbon credit programs provide financial returns for landowners and businesses that restore degraded landscapes. By integrating restoration into regulatory and financial markets, governments help ensure long-term financial sustainability.

Conclusion

Public finance and policy incentives play a foundational role in ecosystem restoration by providing essential funding, regulatory frameworks, and investment incentives. Governments, international institutions, and public agencies contribute significantly to restoration finance through direct funding mechanisms, subsidies, grants, and tax incentives. These financial tools help create an enabling environment for restoration projects, ensuring they are adequately supported and aligned with national and international sustainability goals. However, despite these efforts, public funding alone is insufficient to meet the scale of investment required for large-scale ecosystem restoration.

To bridge this gap, governments increasingly leverage PPPs and blended finance models to attract private sector investment. By reducing financial risks, offering guarantees, and providing co-funding opportunities, public finance helps unlock private capital and expand restoration efforts. Policy incentives such as environmental tax benefits, regulatory mandates, and performance-based subsidies further encourage businesses and investors to integrate restoration into their financial strategies.

Effective governance and transparent financial mechanisms are essential for ensuring that public funds are used efficiently and that restoration projects achieve measurable outcomes. Clear policy frameworks, standardized reporting, and third-party verification systems enhance accountability and build investor confidence. Additionally, aligning restoration finance with broader economic and climate policies ensures long-term sustainability and integration into national development strategies.

While public finance remains a key driver of ecosystem restoration, strengthening its impact requires continued innovation in funding mechanisms, policy alignment, and stakeholder collaboration. By strategically using public resources to catalyze private investment and support sustainable financial models, governments and institutions can scale up restoration efforts, ensuring long-term environmental and economic benefits.

Chapter 3: Market-Based Mechanisms for Ecosystem Restoration Finance

Market-based mechanisms play a growing role in financing ecosystem restoration by leveraging economic incentives to support environmental recovery. Unlike traditional public funding, these approaches integrate restoration into financial markets, creating opportunities for private investment while promoting sustainable land and resource management. By assigning economic value to ecosystem services, market-based mechanisms encourage businesses, investors, and landowners to participate in restoration efforts.

Key financial instruments in this space include carbon markets, PES, biodiversity offsets, and water funds. These mechanisms provide financial returns to those who restore or conserve ecosystems, aligning economic interests with environmental goals. Carbon trading, for example, enables businesses to invest in reforestation projects as part of their emissions reduction commitments, while biodiversity offset programs allow companies to compensate for environmental impacts by funding restoration projects elsewhere.

This chapter explores the role of market-based mechanisms in restoration finance, examining their effectiveness, challenges, and potential for scaling up investment. By integrating restoration into economic systems, these financial tools offer a pathway to sustainable and scalable ecosystem recovery.

Introduction to Market-Based Financial Tools

Market-based financial tools are innovative mechanisms that integrate ecosystem restoration into financial markets, aligning economic incentives with environmental sustainability. These tools provide financial returns for restoration activities by assigning monetary value to ecosystem services such as carbon sequestration, water purification, and biodiversity conservation. Unlike traditional grant-based funding, market-based approaches leverage private sector investment, enabling large-scale restoration efforts while ensuring long-term financial viability.

The Role of Market-Based Mechanisms in Restoration Finance

Market-based financial tools operate on the principle that ecosystems provide valuable services that benefit society and the economy. However, these services are often undervalued or taken for granted, leading to environmental degradation. By establishing financial markets for ecosystem services, these mechanisms create economic incentives for landowners, businesses, and investors to participate in restoration.

Governments, international organizations, and financial institutions are increasingly promoting these mechanisms as a way to mobilize additional resources for restoration projects. Market-based tools also complement public funding by attracting private capital, reducing the financial burden on governments while accelerating restoration efforts.

Types of Market-Based Financial Tools

Several market-based financial instruments support ecosystem restoration:

1. **Carbon Markets** – Carbon trading systems allow businesses and governments to buy and sell carbon credits, which represent the reduction or removal of greenhouse gas emissions. Reforestation and afforestation projects generate carbon credits by sequestering carbon dioxide, providing financial incentives for forest restoration.
2. **PES** – PES programs compensate landowners and communities for maintaining or restoring ecosystems that provide benefits such as clean water, flood prevention, and biodiversity conservation. These payments create direct financial incentives for sustainable land management.

3. **Biodiversity Offsets** – Companies required to mitigate environmental impacts can invest in restoration projects as compensation. This mechanism ensures that economic development does not come at the expense of ecosystem health, promoting sustainable land use.
4. **Water Funds** – Businesses that rely on clean water, such as utilities and beverage companies, invest in upstream watershed restoration to maintain water quality and supply. This approach aligns corporate interests with ecosystem conservation.

Challenges and Opportunities

While market-based mechanisms provide scalable solutions for restoration finance, challenges remain. Establishing financial markets for ecosystem services requires clear regulatory frameworks, strong governance, and standardized measurement systems to ensure transparency and credibility. Additionally, financial returns from restoration investments often take time to materialize, requiring long-term commitments from investors.

Despite these challenges, market-based financial tools present significant opportunities for scaling up restoration. As businesses increasingly prioritize ESG factors, investment in restoration-related financial instruments is expected to grow. By integrating restoration into economic markets, these mechanisms offer a pathway to sustainable and impactful ecosystem recovery.

Carbon Markets and Payments for Ecosystem Services

Carbon markets and PES are two key market-based financial mechanisms that incentivize ecosystem restoration by assigning economic value to environmental benefits. These approaches provide financial returns to landowners, businesses, and governments engaged in conservation and restoration activities, making ecosystem recovery financially viable and scalable.

Carbon Markets and Their Role in Restoration

Carbon markets function as trading systems where businesses, governments, and organizations buy and sell carbon credits to offset their greenhouse gas (GHG) emissions. These credits are generated through projects that remove or reduce carbon dioxide from the atmosphere, including reforestation, afforestation, wetland restoration, and soil carbon sequestration. By linking ecosystem restoration to carbon markets, these financial instruments create economic incentives for preserving and restoring natural landscapes.

There are two main types of carbon markets:

1. **Compliance Carbon Markets** – These are regulated by governments or international agreements, requiring industries and businesses to limit their carbon emissions. Companies exceeding their allowable emissions can purchase carbon credits from restoration projects to remain in compliance. Examples include the European Union Emissions Trading System (EU ETS) and California's Cap-and-Trade Program.
2. **Voluntary Carbon Markets** – In these markets, businesses and individuals purchase carbon credits to meet sustainability commitments beyond regulatory requirements. Voluntary carbon markets have grown as companies seek to reduce their carbon footprints and enhance their ESG performance.

Restoration projects that generate carbon credits must adhere to verification and certification standards, such as the Verified Carbon Standard (VCS) or the Gold Standard, ensuring transparency and credibility. By participating in carbon markets, restoration initiatives can secure long-term funding while contributing to global climate goals.

PES as a Financial Mechanism

PES are financial transactions in which beneficiaries of ecosystem services compensate landowners or communities for maintaining or restoring ecological functions. These programs recognize that ecosystems provide essential services, such as water filtration, biodiversity conservation, and flood prevention, which have economic value. PES schemes create direct financial incentives for sustainable land management and restoration.

Common types of PES programs include:

- **Water-Based PES** – Businesses or municipalities that rely on clean water pay upstream landowners to implement watershed restoration practices, such as reforestation and soil conservation, to improve water quality. Examples include the New York City watershed protection program, where payments support forest conservation to maintain clean drinking water.
- **Biodiversity PES** – Conservation organizations and governments pay landowners to protect habitats critical for endangered species and ecosystem resilience. This approach ensures that biodiversity-rich areas are maintained instead of being converted for agriculture or development.
- **Carbon PES** – Landowners and communities receive financial compensation for maintaining forests and restoring degraded lands that store carbon. These payments often link with carbon markets, where the sale of carbon credits funds long-term restoration activities.

Challenges and Future Prospects

Both carbon markets and PES face challenges, including regulatory complexity, financial uncertainty, and the need for standardized measurement and monitoring systems. Ensuring that carbon credits and PES payments lead to real, additional, and verifiable ecosystem benefits remains critical for their success.

Despite these challenges, these mechanisms present significant opportunities for scaling up restoration finance. As demand for nature-based solutions grows, carbon markets and PES will continue to play a crucial role in funding ecosystem restoration, creating long-term financial incentives for environmental sustainability.

Biodiversity Offsets and Habitat Banking

Biodiversity offsets and habitat banking are market-based financial mechanisms designed to compensate for environmental impacts by restoring, enhancing, or protecting ecosystems elsewhere. These approaches allow governments, businesses, and landowners to mitigate biodiversity loss while ensuring that economic development and conservation goals are balanced. By creating financial incentives for ecosystem restoration, biodiversity offsets and habitat banking help fund large-scale conservation efforts and promote sustainable land management.

Biodiversity Offsets: A Mechanism for Compensation

Biodiversity offsets are conservation actions taken to compensate for the loss of biodiversity caused by development projects, such as infrastructure construction, mining, or urban expansion. These offsets aim to achieve a no net loss or net positive impact on biodiversity by ensuring that any environmental damage is counterbalanced by equivalent or greater restoration elsewhere.

There are two main types of biodiversity offsets:

- **Restoration Offsets** – These involve restoring degraded ecosystems to compensate for habitat destruction caused by a development project. For example, if a company clears a forest for industrial use, it may be required to restore an equivalent area of degraded forest elsewhere.
- **Protection Offsets** – These involve protecting existing ecosystems that are at risk of degradation. A developer may finance the long-term conservation of an ecologically valuable area to offset the biodiversity loss from their project.

Biodiversity offsets are often regulated through national policies or environmental permitting systems, requiring companies to meet offset obligations before proceeding with development. The Business and Biodiversity Offsets Programme (BBOP) provides guidelines for designing and implementing biodiversity offsets, ensuring they are scientifically credible and result in measurable conservation gains.

Habitat Banking: A Market-Driven Conservation Model

Habitat banking is a market-based system that allows developers to purchase conservation credits from entities that restore or protect ecosystems. In this system, restoration or conservation projects generate biodiversity credits, which can then be sold to companies or developers needing to offset their environmental impact.

Habitat banks function similarly to carbon markets, where conservation actions are quantified, certified, and traded. This approach encourages proactive investment in restoration, creating a financial market for biodiversity conservation. Key benefits of habitat banking include:

- **Scalability** – Large-scale restoration projects can be funded by multiple offset buyers, ensuring long-term conservation outcomes.
- **Flexibility** – Developers can purchase biodiversity credits from existing conservation projects instead of directly managing offset sites, reducing administrative and operational burdens.
- **Efficiency** – Habitat banks pool resources to restore and maintain ecosystems more effectively than individual offset projects.

Challenges and Opportunities

Despite their potential, biodiversity offsets and habitat banking face challenges. One concern is ensuring that offsets genuinely compensate for biodiversity loss rather than allowing businesses to justify environmental degradation. Strong regulatory frameworks, transparent monitoring systems, and scientific verification are essential to prevent ineffective or inappropriate offsets.

Additionally, habitat banking requires well-defined markets, standardized crediting mechanisms, and strong governance to ensure its success. Without proper oversight, there is a risk that habitat banks may prioritize financial returns over ecological integrity.

Looking ahead, biodiversity offsets and habitat banking are expected to expand as governments strengthen environmental regulations and businesses prioritize nature-based solutions in their sustainability strategies. By integrating these mechanisms into broader conservation policies, they can provide long-term financial support for ecosystem restoration, ensuring that biodiversity is preserved while economic development continues responsibly.

Conclusion

Market-based mechanisms are increasingly recognized as effective tools for financing ecosystem restoration by aligning economic incentives with environmental objectives. These mechanisms, including carbon markets, biodiversity offsets, and PES, provide financial incentives for businesses, investors, and landowners to participate in restoration efforts. By monetizing the benefits of restored ecosystems, market-driven approaches help attract capital while ensuring that restoration projects generate measurable ecological and economic value.

Carbon markets, in particular, have emerged as a key driver of restoration finance, allowing companies to offset emissions through investments in reforestation, afforestation, and land conservation projects. Similarly, biodiversity credits and habitat banking create financial opportunities for companies to mitigate environmental impacts while contributing to conservation initiatives. These mechanisms enhance the financial viability of restoration projects by establishing revenue streams that support long-term sustainability.

Despite their potential, market-based mechanisms require strong regulatory frameworks, transparent pricing models, and standardized certification systems to ensure credibility and prevent greenwashing. Ensuring the integrity of these financial instruments is essential for maintaining investor confidence and securing long-term funding. Additionally, expanding participation in ecosystem service markets will require greater policy support, improved verification standards, and increased collaboration between governments, businesses, and financial institutions.

While challenges remain, market-based mechanisms represent a scalable and sustainable approach to restoration finance. By integrating restoration into financial markets and investment portfolios, these mechanisms can mobilize significant capital, enhance financial sustainability, and contribute to global conservation efforts. Strengthening governance, expanding market access, and improving impact measurement will be critical to unlocking the full potential of market-driven restoration finance.

Chapter 4: Green Bonds and Sustainable Debt Instruments for Ecosystem Restoration

Green bonds and other sustainable debt instruments are becoming essential tools for financing ecosystem restoration and environmental sustainability. These financial instruments enable governments, corporations, and financial institutions to raise capital specifically for projects that provide environmental benefits, including reforestation, wetland restoration, and biodiversity conservation. By linking capital markets to sustainability objectives, green bonds and sustainable debt instruments help bridge the funding gap for large-scale restoration efforts.

The growing demand for sustainable investment opportunities has led to the expansion of financial products such as blue bonds, sustainability-linked bonds, and debt-for-nature swaps. These instruments provide investors with opportunities to contribute to environmental restoration while ensuring financial returns. At the same time, they help public and private entities access long-term funding for nature-based solutions.

This chapter explores the structure, benefits, and challenges of green bonds and sustainable debt instruments. It examines their role in ecosystem restoration, the evolving market landscape, and strategies for ensuring transparency and accountability in sustainable finance. By leveraging these financial tools, restoration initiatives can achieve greater scale and long-term impact.

Understanding Green, Blue, and Sustainability-Linked Bonds

Green, blue, and sustainability-linked bonds are financial instruments designed to mobilize capital for environmental and sustainability-focused projects. These bonds provide investors with the opportunity to support ecosystem restoration, climate adaptation, and biodiversity conservation while generating financial returns. As the demand for sustainable finance grows, these bonds are playing an increasingly important role in bridging the funding gap for large-scale restoration initiatives.

Green Bonds: Financing Environmental Projects

Green bonds are debt instruments issued by governments, financial institutions, or corporations to fund projects that provide clear environmental benefits. The proceeds from green bonds are exclusively allocated to projects such as reforestation, renewable energy, water conservation, and pollution reduction. These bonds follow recognized frameworks, such as the Green Bond Principles (GBP) set by the International Capital Market Association (ICMA), ensuring transparency and accountability in their use.

Key characteristics of green bonds include:

- **Use of Proceeds** – Funds must be directed toward environmentally beneficial projects.
- **Transparency and Reporting** – Issuers must regularly disclose how proceeds are used.
- **Third-Party Verification** – External assessments ensure compliance with sustainability goals.

Green bonds have gained global traction, with governments and corporations using them to finance large-scale restoration efforts. They help attract institutional investors focused on sustainable finance, making them a key tool for expanding restoration funding.

Blue Bonds: Supporting Ocean and Water Conservation

Blue bonds function similarly to green bonds but are specifically designed to finance projects related to ocean and freshwater conservation. Issued by governments, development banks, or corporations, blue bonds support marine ecosystem restoration, sustainable fisheries, coastal protection, and water resource management.

Key applications of blue bonds include:

3. **Coral Reef Restoration** – Funding projects that protect and restore marine biodiversity.
4. **Sustainable Fisheries** – Supporting responsible fishing practices that maintain ecosystem balance.
5. **Coastal Infrastructure Resilience** – Financing projects that protect coastlines from erosion and rising sea levels.

One of the most notable examples is the Seychelles Blue Bond, issued in partnership with the World Bank to support sustainable fisheries and marine conservation. Blue bonds are becoming an essential tool in financing nature-based solutions that address climate change and biodiversity loss in marine environments.

Sustainability-Linked Bonds: A Performance-Based Approach

Unlike green and blue bonds, sustainability-linked bonds (SLBs) do not require proceeds to be allocated to specific environmental projects. Instead, SLBs are tied to an issuer's broader sustainability performance, with financial terms linked to the achievement of predefined environmental, social, or governance (ESG) targets. If the issuer fails to meet sustainability goals—such as reducing carbon emissions, restoring degraded land, or increasing renewable energy use—penalties such as higher interest rates may apply.

Key advantages of sustainability-linked bonds:

- **Flexibility** – Funds can be used for general corporate purposes while still promoting sustainability.
- **Accountability** – Issuers are incentivized to meet ESG commitments.
- **Scalability** – Encourages companies across various sectors to integrate sustainability into operations.

SLBs have gained popularity among corporations and financial institutions looking to enhance their sustainability credentials. By linking financial performance to environmental outcomes, they encourage long-term investment in ecosystem restoration and climate adaptation.

Role of Multilateral Institutions and Investors

Multilateral institutions and investors play a crucial role in financing ecosystem restoration through green bonds and other sustainable debt instruments. By providing capital, risk mitigation, and technical expertise, these entities help mobilize large-scale funding for environmental projects. Their involvement ensures that restoration efforts align with global sustainability goals while creating financial opportunities for investors.

Multilateral Institutions as Catalysts for Sustainable Finance

Multilateral institutions, such as the World Bank, International Monetary Fund (IMF), ADB, Inter-American Development Bank (IDB), and the GCF, play a leading role in structuring and financing green and blue bonds. These institutions support ecosystem restoration by:

- **Issuing Bonds** – Many multilateral banks issue green and blue bonds to raise capital for large-scale environmental projects. For example, the World Bank has issued billions in green bonds to finance climate resilience, reforestation, and water conservation efforts.
- **Providing Technical Assistance** – Institutions such as the GEF and the UN Environment Programme (UNEP) offer technical expertise to help governments and organizations develop restoration projects that meet financial and environmental criteria.
- **De-Risking Investments** – By offering guarantees, concessional loans, or blended finance mechanisms, these institutions reduce investment risks and encourage private

sector participation. They help ensure that sustainable projects are financially viable and attractive to investors.

- **Aligning Projects with Global Commitments** – Multilateral institutions ensure that investments in restoration finance contribute to broader sustainability targets, such as the Paris Agreement, the UN SDGs, and the Convention on Biological Diversity (CBD).

By playing these roles, multilateral institutions help bridge financial gaps, making it easier for countries and organizations to access capital for ecosystem restoration.

Institutional Investors and Sustainable Finance

Institutional investors, including pension funds, asset managers, sovereign wealth funds, and insurance companies, are increasingly integrating ESG factors into their investment strategies. The growing demand for sustainable investments has led to a significant rise in green, blue, and sustainability-linked bonds, providing new financial pathways for ecosystem restoration.

Key ways institutional investors support restoration finance include:

- **Purchasing Green and Blue Bonds** – Institutional investors buy these bonds as part of their sustainability-oriented portfolios, providing capital for nature-based projects.
- **Engaging in Impact Investing** – Some investors allocate funds directly to projects that generate measurable environmental and financial returns, such as afforestation, wetland restoration, and biodiversity conservation.
- **Supporting ESG Integration** – Many institutional investors apply ESG screening criteria when selecting investment opportunities, prioritizing bonds that contribute to long-term sustainability.
- **Advocating for Policy and Regulatory Improvements** – Large investors influence financial regulations and market

standards, promoting transparency, accountability, and best practices in sustainable finance.

Public-Private Partnerships for Restoration Finance

Multilateral institutions and investors often collaborate through PPPs to fund large-scale restoration projects. By combining public sector funding with private capital, PPPs leverage financial resources more effectively and create long-term investment opportunities.

For example, the GCF frequently partners with development banks and institutional investors to finance restoration projects in climate-vulnerable regions. Similarly, sovereign green bond issuances attract institutional capital while aligning national policies with global sustainability targets.

Debt-for-Nature Swaps and Large-Scale Restoration

Debt-for-nature swaps are an innovative financial mechanism that allows countries to reduce their external debt in exchange for commitments to environmental conservation and ecosystem restoration. These agreements, typically involving governments, creditors, and conservation organizations, help unlock funding for large-scale restoration while easing financial burdens on debt-laden nations. By linking debt relief to environmental sustainability, debt-for-nature swaps create long-term financial incentives for conservation efforts.

How Debt-for-Nature Swaps Work

In a typical debt-for-nature swap, a portion of a country's external debt is purchased, restructured, or forgiven by a creditor—often a foreign government, multilateral institution, or private lender. In return, the debtor country agrees to allocate an equivalent amount in local currency to finance conservation and restoration projects. These funds are typically directed toward initiatives such as:

- Reforestation and afforestation to restore degraded landscapes.
- Biodiversity conservation through protected area management.
- Wetland and coastal ecosystem restoration to enhance climate resilience.
- Sustainable land-use practices that prevent further environmental degradation.

Debt-for-nature swaps provide financial relief while ensuring that conservation becomes a national priority. They are particularly beneficial for countries with high biodiversity and natural resources at risk but limited financial capacity to fund large-scale restoration independently.

Examples of Debt-for-Nature Swaps

Several countries have successfully implemented debt-for-nature swaps to fund restoration and conservation:

- **Seychelles (2016)** – The government restructured $21.6 million of its national debt in exchange for commitments to marine conservation, creating protected areas covering 30% of its ocean territory. This swap was facilitated by The Nature Conservancy and financed by philanthropic donors and international lenders.
- **Costa Rica (2007, 2010)** – The country engaged in multiple debt-for-nature swaps with the U.S. government, channeling funds into reforestation, watershed protection, and biodiversity conservation. These agreements strengthened Costa Rica's position as a global leader in sustainable development.
- **Indonesia (2011)** – The U.S. and Indonesia agreed on a $28.5 million debt swap to support tropical forest conservation and carbon sequestration efforts, benefiting both biodiversity and climate mitigation.

These examples highlight the ability of debt-for-nature swaps to facilitate large-scale restoration while strengthening economic and environmental resilience.

Challenges and Considerations

Despite their benefits, debt-for-nature swaps face several challenges:

1. **Complex Negotiations** – These agreements require collaboration between multiple stakeholders, including governments, financial institutions, and conservation organizations, making the process lengthy and complex.
2. **Debt Market Constraints** – Countries with limited debt eligible for restructuring may struggle to secure meaningful financial relief through swaps.
3. **Long-Term Governance** – Ensuring that funds are used effectively for restoration projects requires strong governance, transparency, and accountability mechanisms.

To maximize the impact of debt-for-nature swaps, governments and financial institutions must integrate them into broader sustainable finance strategies, ensuring that conservation commitments translate into measurable environmental outcomes.

Challenges and Opportunities in Debt Instruments

Debt instruments, including green bonds, blue bonds, sustainability-linked bonds, and debt-for-nature swaps, have become essential tools for financing ecosystem restoration. These financial mechanisms enable governments, corporations, and financial institutions to mobilize capital for large-scale environmental projects. However, despite their potential, debt instruments face challenges that must be addressed to maximize their impact. At the same time, growing market demand and policy support present opportunities to expand their use in restoration finance.

Challenges in Debt Instruments for Restoration

1. **Regulatory and Market Barriers** – Sustainable debt instruments require clear regulatory frameworks to ensure transparency, accountability, and proper use of funds. In many regions, inconsistent policies and a lack of standardization make it difficult for investors to assess the credibility of restoration-related bonds. Without strong oversight, there is a risk of "greenwashing," where funds are not effectively directed toward environmental projects.
2. **High Transaction Costs and Complexity** – Issuing green or blue bonds involves extensive due diligence, third-party verification, and impact reporting. These processes increase administrative costs and may deter smaller organizations or governments with limited financial resources from participating in the market.
3. **Long-Term Financial Risks** – Many restoration projects funded through debt instruments require years, or even decades, to generate measurable environmental and financial returns. Investors seeking short-term gains may be hesitant to commit capital to bonds with extended payback periods, limiting market expansion.
4. **Limited Market Liquidity** – Compared to traditional financial instruments, sustainable debt markets remain relatively small. The lack of secondary markets for green and blue bonds can make it difficult for investors to trade these assets, reducing their attractiveness compared to conventional bonds.

Opportunities for Expanding Sustainable Debt Instruments

1. **Growing Investor Demand** – Institutional investors, including pension funds and asset managers, are increasingly prioritizing ESG factors. This trend is driving demand for sustainable bonds, creating new funding opportunities for ecosystem restoration.
2. **Stronger Policy Support** – Governments and multilateral institutions are strengthening regulatory frameworks and providing incentives to encourage sustainable bond issuance.

Increased public-private collaboration can further enhance
market stability and investor confidence.
3. **Financial Innovation** – New financial structures, such as
blended finance models and sustainability-linked bonds, are
making debt instruments more adaptable to restoration
projects. These innovations reduce risks and attract a broader
range of investors.

Conclusion

Green bonds and sustainable debt instruments play a vital role in
financing ecosystem restoration by providing long-term capital for
large-scale environmental projects. As the demand for sustainable
finance grows, these instruments offer a structured approach to
raising funds for restoration efforts while aligning financial returns
with environmental benefits. Governments, corporations, and
financial institutions are increasingly leveraging green bonds, blue
bonds, and sustainability-linked debt instruments to mobilize capital
for nature-based solutions.

Green bonds, in particular, have proven to be an effective tool for
directing investments toward reforestation, watershed management,
and biodiversity conservation. Their structured financial model
allows issuers to raise capital while ensuring that funds are allocated
to environmentally sustainable projects. Similarly, sustainability-
linked bonds and loans provide flexibility by linking financial terms
to specific environmental performance indicators, encouraging long-
term investment in restoration initiatives.

Debt-for-nature swaps offer another innovative approach by
restructuring sovereign debt in exchange for commitments to
conservation and restoration. These agreements enable countries to
prioritize environmental investments while addressing financial
obligations, creating mutually beneficial outcomes for economic
stability and ecological sustainability. However, despite their
potential, scaling up these financial instruments requires stronger
regulatory frameworks, investor confidence, and transparency in
impact reporting.

Ensuring the long-term success of green bonds and sustainable debt instruments depends on clear standards, independent verification, and accountability mechanisms. Strengthening governance structures, increasing market participation, and integrating these instruments into broader financial strategies will be essential for expanding restoration finance. As sustainable finance continues to evolve, green bonds and debt instruments will remain key mechanisms for mobilizing large-scale investments, bridging financial gaps, and supporting the transition to a more resilient and sustainable future.

Chapter 5: Impact Investment and Blended Finance for Ecosystem Restoration

Impact investment and blended finance have emerged as effective strategies for mobilizing capital toward ecosystem restoration while balancing financial returns with positive environmental and social outcomes. These approaches attract both public and private sector funding by creating investment opportunities that generate measurable sustainability benefits.

Impact investment focuses on directing capital toward projects that deliver positive environmental impact alongside financial returns. Investors in this space prioritize nature-based solutions, sustainable agriculture, and climate resilience initiatives, making impact investment a key driver of ecosystem restoration finance.

Blended finance, on the other hand, combines public and private funding sources to de-risk investments in restoration. By leveraging concessional capital from governments, multilateral institutions, or philanthropic sources, blended finance structures encourage private sector participation in projects that might otherwise be considered too risky or unprofitable.

This chapter explores the principles of impact investment and blended finance, their role in funding restoration projects, and the challenges and opportunities associated with scaling these financial mechanisms. By integrating these approaches into sustainable finance strategies, restoration initiatives can attract long-term investment and achieve greater environmental impact.

Definition and Rise of Impact Investing

Impact investing is a financial approach that seeks to generate measurable environmental and social benefits alongside financial returns. Unlike traditional investments that prioritize profit maximization, impact investing integrates sustainability considerations into investment decisions, directing capital toward projects that address global challenges such as climate change, biodiversity loss, and ecosystem degradation.

Defining Impact Investing

Impact investing is distinct from philanthropy and CSR in that it actively seeks both financial gains and positive environmental outcomes. Investors in this space expect market-rate or concessionary returns while ensuring that their investments contribute to sustainability objectives. Impact investments typically fund projects related to:

- **Ecosystem restoration** – Reforestation, wetland rehabilitation, and sustainable land management.
- **Climate resilience** – Nature-based solutions to mitigate climate risks and enhance carbon sequestration.
- **Sustainable agriculture and forestry** – Regenerative farming practices and responsible forestry management.
- **Water and biodiversity conservation** – Projects that protect freshwater ecosystems and restore wildlife habitats.

The success of impact investments is measured through ESG metrics and sustainability indicators. These assessments ensure that capital is effectively deployed to achieve tangible environmental improvements.

The Rise of Impact Investing

Impact investing has gained momentum over the past two decades due to increasing awareness of environmental challenges, stronger policy support, and evolving investor preferences. Several factors have contributed to the rapid expansion of this financial model:

6. **Shifting Investor Priorities** – Institutional investors, asset managers, and pension funds are increasingly integrating ESG considerations into their portfolios. Many investors recognize that environmental sustainability is linked to long-term financial stability, making impact investing a strategic choice for risk mitigation and value creation.

7. **Policy and Regulatory Support** – Governments and international organizations have introduced policies that promote sustainable investment. Frameworks such as the **EU** Sustainable Finance Disclosure Regulation (SFDR) and the Task Force on Climate-related Financial Disclosures (TCFD) encourage transparency in ESG reporting, making it easier for investors to identify and support impact-driven projects.

8. **Growth of Green Financial Instruments** – The expansion of green bonds, sustainability-linked loans, and conservation finance mechanisms has provided new opportunities for impact investors. These financial instruments facilitate capital flows into restoration initiatives while offering predictable returns.

9. **Corporate Commitments to ESG Goals** – Many multinational corporations have set ambitious sustainability targets, leading them to engage in impact investing. Businesses invest in ecosystem restoration projects as part of their carbon offset strategies, biodiversity conservation programs, and corporate sustainability efforts.

10. **Technological Advancements and Data Transparency** – Digital tools, remote sensing, and blockchain technology have improved the ability to track and verify the impact of investments. These innovations enhance investor confidence by ensuring accountability in sustainability projects.

Future of Impact Investing in Ecosystem Restoration

As environmental concerns continue to grow, impact investing is expected to play an even greater role in funding large-scale restoration projects. The development of standardized impact measurement frameworks, enhanced policy incentives, and financial innovations will further drive capital toward nature-based solutions.

By aligning financial interests with ecological sustainability, impact investing creates opportunities for long-term ecosystem resilience, economic growth, and social well-being. Its expansion represents a shift toward a more responsible and forward-thinking financial system that supports global restoration goals.

Blended Finance Models for Restoration

Blended finance is an investment approach that combines public, private, and philanthropic funding to mobilize capital for projects that deliver environmental, social, and financial benefits. It is particularly useful for financing ecosystem restoration, where traditional investments may not be viable due to long payback periods, perceived risks, or uncertain financial returns. By strategically using public and concessional capital to reduce investment risks, blended finance helps attract private sector funding for large-scale restoration projects.

How Blended Finance Works

Blended finance structures typically involve a mix of funding sources, each playing a distinct role in supporting restoration initiatives. The main components include:

- **Public and Multilateral Funding** – Governments, development banks, and international financial institutions provide grants, concessional loans, or guarantees to de-risk restoration investments.
- **Private Sector Investment** – Corporations, asset managers, and institutional investors contribute commercial capital to restoration projects, leveraging public funds for additional financing.
- **Philanthropic Contributions** – Nonprofit organizations, foundations, and impact investors provide seed funding,

technical assistance, or capacity-building support to enhance project viability.

By aligning financial incentives with conservation goals, blended finance makes restoration projects more attractive to investors who might otherwise perceive them as too risky or unprofitable.

Key Blended Finance Mechanisms

Several blended finance models support ecosystem restoration:

- **Grants and Concessional Loans** – Public and philanthropic funds provide early-stage capital to cover project development costs, making investments more viable for private sector participation.
- **Guarantees and Risk Mitigation Instruments** – Credit guarantees, political risk insurance, and partial loan guarantees reduce financial risks for private investors, encouraging long-term commitments.
- **PPPs** – Governments and businesses collaborate on restoration projects, sharing financial risks and operational responsibilities. PPPs help scale up nature-based solutions by integrating market-driven approaches with policy support.
- **Impact Investment Funds** – Pooled capital from public, private, and philanthropic sources finances multiple restoration projects, diversifying risks and maximizing impact.
- **Performance-Based Financing** – Investors receive returns based on environmental outcomes, such as carbon sequestration, biodiversity conservation, or improved water quality.

Advantages and Challenges

Blended finance provides several benefits for restoration projects:

- **Increases Financial Scale** – By leveraging public and private funds, blended finance mobilizes greater capital for restoration than traditional funding models.
- **Reduces Investment Risks** – Public and concessional financing de-risks investments, making ecosystem restoration attractive to commercial investors.
- **Enhances Sustainability** – Long-term funding structures ensure that restoration projects maintain financial stability beyond initial implementation.

However, challenges remain, including:

- **Complex Deal Structuring** – Blended finance transactions require coordination between multiple stakeholders, which can be time-consuming and administratively complex.
- **Regulatory Barriers** – Differences in legal and policy frameworks can complicate cross-sector partnerships and financing mechanisms.
- **Measuring Impact** – Standardized metrics for tracking ecological and financial performance are needed to ensure transparency and accountability.

Natural Capital Investment Funds

Natural capital investment funds are financial instruments designed to mobilize capital for projects that enhance ecosystem health, biodiversity, and sustainable land use. These funds operate by attracting investments from institutional investors, governments, philanthropic organizations, and private enterprises to finance large-scale restoration and conservation initiatives. By valuing natural ecosystems as productive assets, natural capital investment funds provide a structured approach to sustainable finance, ensuring long-term ecological and economic benefits.

Understanding Natural Capital Investment Funds

Natural capital refers to the world's stock of natural resources, including forests, wetlands, oceans, and soil, which provide essential ecosystem services such as carbon sequestration, water filtration, and biodiversity conservation. Investment funds dedicated to natural capital seek to generate financial returns while restoring and protecting these valuable assets.

Unlike traditional conservation funding, which often relies on government grants and philanthropy, natural capital investment funds operate on a market-based model, encouraging private sector participation. Investors in these funds can achieve both financial and environmental returns, making them an attractive option for sustainability-focused asset managers and institutional investors.

Types of Natural Capital Investment Funds

There are several types of natural capital investment funds, each focusing on different aspects of ecosystem restoration and conservation:

- **Sustainable Forestry Funds** – These funds invest in reforestation, afforestation, and responsible forest management practices to generate returns through timber production, carbon credits, and biodiversity conservation.
- **Agricultural Investment Funds** – Focused on regenerative agriculture and sustainable farming practices, these funds finance soil restoration, water-efficient irrigation systems, and agroforestry initiatives.
- **Blue Economy Funds** – Targeting marine and coastal ecosystems, these funds support sustainable fisheries, coral reef restoration, and ocean-based carbon sequestration projects.
- **Biodiversity Conservation Funds** – Dedicated to protecting endangered species and restoring habitats, these funds often work through biodiversity offset programs and conservation finance mechanisms.

How Natural Capital Funds Generate Returns

Natural capital investment funds generate financial returns through various revenue streams, including:

4. **Carbon Markets** – Funds invest in reforestation and soil restoration projects that generate carbon credits, which can be sold in compliance or voluntary carbon markets.
5. **PES** – Landowners and businesses receive compensation for maintaining natural ecosystems that provide valuable services, such as water purification and flood prevention.
6. **Sustainable Resource Management** – Funds invest in responsible forestry, agriculture, and fisheries that generate long-term revenue while maintaining ecological integrity.
7. **Eco-Tourism and Conservation Enterprises** – Some funds support nature-based tourism and sustainable business models that provide economic incentives for conservation.

Challenges and Opportunities

Despite their potential, natural capital investment funds face several challenges:

5. **Market Development** – Many investors are unfamiliar with natural capital as an asset class, requiring greater awareness and education.
6. **Regulatory Barriers** – Unclear policies and inconsistent legal frameworks can create uncertainties for investors.
7. **Measuring Impact** – Standardized metrics are needed to evaluate the environmental and financial performance of investments.

However, opportunities for growth in natural capital finance are expanding:

4. **Increasing Investor Demand** – Institutional investors and corporations are integrating ESG factors into their portfolios, driving demand for sustainable investments.
5. **Policy and Regulatory Support** – Governments and multilateral institutions are creating incentives and frameworks to support natural capital investment.
6. **Financial Innovation** – New financial instruments, such as green bonds and sustainability-linked loans, are improving access to capital for nature-based solutions.

Measuring Impact and Financial Returns

Measuring the impact and financial returns of ecosystem restoration investments is essential for ensuring accountability, attracting investors, and demonstrating long-term sustainability benefits. Unlike traditional financial investments, restoration projects generate both economic and environmental value, requiring a combination of financial performance metrics and sustainability indicators. Clear and transparent measurement frameworks help investors assess the viability and success of their investments while ensuring that restoration projects achieve their intended ecological outcomes.

Key Environmental Impact Metrics

Impact measurement in restoration finance involves tracking key ecological indicators that demonstrate progress toward sustainability goals. Common metrics include:

- **Carbon Sequestration** – Measured in metric tons of CO_2 captured, this metric assesses the effectiveness of afforestation, reforestation, and soil restoration projects in mitigating climate change.
- **Biodiversity Gains** – Monitored through species diversity, habitat restoration, and population recovery of key species, biodiversity metrics track improvements in ecosystem health.

- **Water Quality and Availability** – Restoration projects impacting watersheds or wetlands measure changes in water filtration, groundwater recharge, and pollution reduction.
- **Soil Health and Land Productivity** – Assessed through soil carbon content, erosion rates, and fertility improvements, these indicators evaluate the long-term benefits of sustainable land management.

Financial Return Metrics

In addition to environmental impact, investors assess financial returns to ensure economic viability. Common financial performance indicators include:

- **Return on Investment (ROI)** – Measures profitability by comparing investment costs to financial returns generated through sustainable land use, carbon credit sales, or resource-based revenue.
- **Revenue from Ecosystem Services** – Tracks income generated from PES, sustainable forestry, biodiversity credits, and conservation-based tourism.
- **Asset Appreciation** – Evaluates the long-term value increase of restored land and natural assets, contributing to financial stability.
- **Blended Finance Leverage Ratio** – Measures the ratio of private investment mobilized for every dollar of public or concessional finance, indicating the effectiveness of financial structuring.

Challenges and Standardization

Despite advancements in impact measurement, challenges remain in standardizing methodologies across different restoration projects. Varying ecosystems, financial models, and regulatory frameworks create inconsistencies in reporting. However, organizations such as the Global Impact Investing Network (GIIN) and Taskforce on Nature-related Financial Disclosures (TNFD) are working to

establish standardized metrics that enhance transparency and
comparability.

Conclusion

Impact investment and blended finance are key strategies for
mobilizing private capital to support large-scale ecosystem
restoration. These approaches attract investors seeking both financial
returns and measurable environmental benefits, ensuring that
restoration projects receive the necessary funding to achieve long-
term sustainability. By combining public, private, and philanthropic
capital, impact investment and blended finance create opportunities
to scale up restoration efforts while distributing financial risks
among multiple stakeholders.

Impact investing has gained momentum as businesses and
institutional investors recognize the value of financing projects that
contribute to biodiversity conservation, climate resilience, and
ecosystem recovery. Investors are increasingly integrating nature-
based solutions into their portfolios, driven by ESG commitments.
This shift not only supports ecological restoration but also
strengthens the business case for sustainable investment by
demonstrating the long-term economic value of natural capital.

Blended finance further enhances the feasibility of restoration
projects by leveraging concessional funding from governments,
development banks, and philanthropic organizations to de-risk
private sector investments. This model encourages private investors
to engage in restoration finance by reducing perceived financial risks
and improving the overall attractiveness of nature-based projects. By
combining different sources of capital, blended finance ensures that
restoration initiatives remain financially viable while delivering
significant environmental and social benefits.

However, scaling impact investment and blended finance requires
robust governance, standardized impact measurement, and stronger
policy support. Investors need clear frameworks to assess financial

risks and ecological outcomes, while regulatory incentives can further encourage private sector participation. Strengthening multi-stakeholder collaboration and integrating these financial models into mainstream investment strategies will be essential for closing funding gaps and expanding restoration finance.

As financial markets increasingly align with sustainability goals, impact investment and blended finance will remain critical tools for mobilizing capital, promoting environmental resilience, and ensuring that restoration efforts contribute to a more sustainable global economy.

Chapter 6: Corporate and Philanthropic Investment in Ecosystem Restoration

Corporate and philanthropic investment plays a significant role in financing ecosystem restoration, complementing public funding and market-based mechanisms. As businesses recognize the financial and reputational benefits of sustainability, many are integrating restoration efforts into their CSR and ESG strategies. Companies invest in restoration to mitigate environmental risks, meet regulatory requirements, and enhance brand value through sustainable practices.

Philanthropic organizations, including foundations, impact-driven funds, and high-net-worth individuals, also contribute substantially to restoration efforts. Unlike corporate investments, which often seek measurable financial returns, philanthropic funding prioritizes long-term environmental and social benefits. Grants, donations, and endowments help finance critical restoration initiatives that may not attract commercial investment, supporting biodiversity conservation, climate resilience, and sustainable land management.

This chapter explores how corporate and philanthropic investments drive restoration finance, the motivations behind these contributions, and the opportunities and challenges associated with scaling private-sector engagement. By leveraging corporate and philanthropic capital, restoration efforts can achieve greater impact and long-term sustainability.

Corporate Sustainability Strategies and ESG-Driven Funding

Corporate sustainability strategies have become central to business operations as companies recognize the long-term benefits of integrating ESG principles into their decision-making. Ecosystem restoration is increasingly included in corporate sustainability initiatives, as businesses seek to mitigate environmental risks, comply with regulatory frameworks, and enhance their reputations. ESG-driven funding enables corporations to allocate financial resources toward restoration efforts while aligning their business strategies with global sustainability goals.

Corporate Motivation for Investing in Restoration

Businesses engage in restoration efforts for several reasons, including:

1. **Regulatory Compliance** – Many governments require companies to mitigate environmental impacts through restoration or offset initiatives. Compliance with environmental laws, such as biodiversity offset policies and carbon reduction targets, incentivizes businesses to invest in restoration projects.
2. **Risk Management** – Industries that rely on natural resources, such as agriculture, forestry, and water utilities, invest in ecosystem restoration to secure long-term resource availability and climate resilience.
3. **Reputation and Brand Value** – Consumers and investors increasingly favor companies that demonstrate environmental responsibility. By funding restoration projects, businesses enhance their corporate image and build stronger relationships with stakeholders.
4. **Carbon Offsetting and Climate Commitments** – Many corporations have set net-zero emissions goals, driving investments in nature-based solutions such as reforestation and wetland restoration to offset their carbon footprints.
5. **Market Differentiation and Competitive Advantage** – Companies integrating sustainability into their core business strategy gain a competitive edge by meeting evolving market demands for environmentally responsible products and services.

ESG-Driven Funding Mechanisms

Corporate ESG funding for restoration takes multiple forms, including direct investments, sustainability-linked financing, and participation in environmental markets.

11. **Green and Sustainability-Linked Bonds** – Many corporations issue green bonds to raise capital for restoration projects. SLBs tie financial incentives to environmental performance targets, such as restoring degraded landscapes or reducing carbon emissions.

12. **Corporate Grants and Impact Investing** – Some businesses establish corporate foundations or impact investment funds to support ecosystem restoration initiatives. These funds provide financial resources to NGOs, community-led conservation efforts, and research institutions.

13. **Carbon Markets and Offsetting Programs** – Companies purchase carbon credits generated from reforestation, afforestation, and soil carbon sequestration projects, integrating ecosystem restoration into their sustainability strategies.

14. **PPPs** – Businesses collaborate with governments and conservation organizations to co-finance large-scale restoration projects, leveraging shared resources for greater environmental impact.

15. **Biodiversity Offsets and Conservation Finance** – Companies in sectors such as mining, infrastructure, and real estate invest in biodiversity offsets to compensate for environmental impacts, funding habitat restoration and conservation programs.

Challenges and Considerations

Despite the growing role of corporate funding in restoration, challenges remain:

- **Greenwashing Risks** – Some businesses engage in superficial sustainability initiatives without making meaningful environmental commitments. Ensuring transparency and accountability in ESG-driven funding is critical for credibility.

- **Long-Term Financial Commitment** – Ecosystem restoration requires sustained investment over time, but many businesses operate on short-term financial cycles. Maintaining long-term funding strategies is essential for project success.
- **Measuring Impact and ROI** – Defining clear metrics for environmental and financial performance helps businesses track the effectiveness of restoration investments and demonstrate measurable benefits to investors and stakeholders.
- **Regulatory and Market Uncertainty** – Evolving ESG regulations and financial market fluctuations can influence corporate investment decisions, requiring adaptive strategies for long-term sustainability.

Role of Philanthropic Foundations and Environmental Endowments

Philanthropic foundations and environmental endowments play a crucial role in financing ecosystem restoration by providing long-term funding for conservation, biodiversity protection, and sustainable land management. Unlike market-based financial instruments that seek direct financial returns, philanthropic funding focuses on maximizing environmental and social benefits. These funds help bridge financial gaps in restoration projects that may not attract commercial investment, ensuring that critical conservation initiatives receive the necessary resources for long-term success.

Philanthropic Foundations as Key Contributors

Philanthropic foundations support ecosystem restoration through grants, donations, and strategic funding programs. These foundations typically focus on addressing global environmental challenges, such as deforestation, land degradation, and climate change adaptation. Their contributions often target projects that align with broader conservation goals, including habitat restoration, sustainable agriculture, and carbon sequestration.

- **Direct Funding for Restoration Projects** – Many foundations provide direct financial support to restoration initiatives, funding reforestation programs, wetland rehabilitation, and soil conservation efforts. These funds enable NGOs, research institutions, and local communities to implement large-scale restoration activities.
- **Capacity Building and Technical Assistance** – In addition to financial support, foundations invest in capacity-building programs, helping local stakeholders develop the technical expertise and infrastructure needed to sustain restoration efforts over time.
- **Innovation and Research Grants** – Some philanthropic organizations fund research on ecological restoration, climate adaptation, and sustainable land-use practices, fostering innovation and evidence-based approaches to conservation.
- **Community-Based Restoration Initiatives** – Many foundations prioritize funding for projects led by indigenous and local communities, ensuring that restoration efforts align with traditional knowledge and promote social inclusion.

Notable philanthropic organizations involved in restoration finance include the David and Lucile Packard Foundation, the Gordon and Betty Moore Foundation, and the Bezos Earth Fund, all of which allocate significant funding to ecosystem conservation and biodiversity protection.

Environmental Endowments and Long-Term Funding

Environmental endowments are financial assets specifically set aside to provide long-term funding for conservation and restoration initiatives. These funds generate income through investments, ensuring continuous financial support for environmental projects.

- **Permanently Restricted Endowments** – These endowments invest principal funds while using only the generated income to finance restoration projects, ensuring sustained long-term funding.
- **Quasi-Endowments** – These funds allow for flexibility in spending, enabling organizations to allocate financial resources according to conservation priorities and emerging environmental challenges.
- **Pooled Conservation Funds** – Some endowments consolidate resources from multiple donors, creating larger investment pools that finance large-scale restoration efforts.

Endowments are managed by conservation organizations, universities, and non-profits, providing a stable financial foundation for long-term restoration commitments. Examples include The Nature Conservancy's endowment fund and the World Wildlife Fund's (WWF) Global Conservation Fund, both of which support biodiversity conservation and ecosystem restoration worldwide.

Challenges and Opportunities in Philanthropic and Endowment Funding

While philanthropic funding and environmental endowments play a vital role in restoration finance, they face several challenges:

- **Limited Scale Compared to Market-Based Mechanisms** – While philanthropy provides critical funding, it often lacks the scale and leverage of private sector investments, making it essential to integrate these funds with other financial mechanisms.
- **Dependence on Donor Priorities** – Funding availability can fluctuate based on donor interests and economic conditions, creating uncertainty for long-term restoration projects.
- **Ensuring Financial Sustainability** – Endowments require careful financial management to generate consistent income while maintaining their principal value.

Despite these challenges, opportunities for expanding philanthropic funding in restoration are growing:

- **Blended Finance Models** – Philanthropic capital is increasingly being used in blended finance structures, where it helps de-risk investments and attract private sector funding.
- **Strategic Partnerships** – Collaboration between foundations, governments, and financial institutions can amplify the impact of philanthropic funding by integrating it into broader conservation finance strategies.
- **Greater Public Awareness** – Rising global attention on biodiversity loss and climate change has led to increased philanthropic commitments to ecosystem restoration.

Corporate Partnerships for Restoration Financing

Corporate partnerships play a crucial role in financing ecosystem restoration by leveraging business resources, expertise, and networks to support large-scale environmental initiatives. As sustainability becomes an integral part of corporate strategies, businesses are increasingly collaborating with governments, NGOs, and financial institutions to fund and implement restoration projects. These partnerships provide financial support, drive innovation, and enhance the scalability of restoration efforts while helping companies meet ESG goals.

Types of Corporate Partnerships in Restoration Finance

Corporate partnerships for restoration financing take several forms, including direct investments, co-financing agreements, and multi-stakeholder collaborations. These partnerships enable businesses to align financial commitments with long-term sustainability objectives while contributing to global environmental goals.

8. **PPPs** – Companies collaborate with governments and international organizations to co-finance restoration projects. These partnerships reduce financial risks by sharing costs,

ensuring that restoration efforts align with national and regional sustainability policies. For example, businesses in the agriculture, forestry, and water sectors partner with public entities to restore degraded land and watersheds.

9. **Corporate-NGO Collaborations** – Many companies partner with conservation organizations and environmental NGOs to implement restoration projects. NGOs provide technical expertise, while corporations contribute funding and logistical support. Such collaborations often focus on habitat restoration, biodiversity conservation, and community-led initiatives.

10. **Industry Consortiums and Alliances** – Businesses within the same industry form coalitions to collectively finance restoration projects. These partnerships enable companies to pool resources, share best practices, and create industry-wide sustainability standards. Examples include global forestry initiatives that promote reforestation and sustainable land management.

11. **Supply Chain Sustainability Initiatives** – Corporations integrate restoration financing into their supply chain operations, ensuring that sourcing practices contribute to environmental recovery. Companies in the food, fashion, and consumer goods industries invest in sustainable agriculture, responsible forestry, and water conservation programs to enhance supply chain resilience.

12. **Carbon Offset and Biodiversity Credit Programs** – Businesses invest in restoration projects that generate carbon credits or biodiversity offsets to meet regulatory requirements and voluntary sustainability commitments. These investments help companies achieve carbon neutrality and offset ecological impacts from operations.

Benefits of Corporate Partnerships in Restoration

Corporate partnerships provide multiple advantages for ecosystem restoration and long-term sustainability.

8. **Financial Stability and Scale** – Businesses bring financial resources that complement public funding, enabling large-scale restoration projects to secure long-term investment.
9. **Innovation and Technology** – Companies contribute expertise in research, digital tools, and data analysis to improve restoration outcomes and project efficiency.
10.   **Brand Reputation and Consumer Trust** – Engaging in restoration initiatives enhances corporate reputation, demonstrating environmental responsibility to customers, investors, and stakeholders.
11.   **Regulatory Compliance and Risk Mitigation** – Investing in restoration helps businesses comply with environmental regulations, manage operational risks, and secure long-term access to natural resources.

Challenges in Corporate Partnerships for Restoration

Despite the benefits, corporate partnerships in restoration financing face several challenges:

7. **Greenwashing Concerns** – Some companies engage in restoration projects primarily for public relations benefits rather than genuine environmental impact. Ensuring transparency, accountability, and measurable results is critical.
8. **Long-Term Commitment Issues** – Restoration efforts require sustained investment, but businesses often operate on short-term financial cycles, making long-term funding commitments challenging.
9. **Regulatory and Policy Barriers** – Inconsistent policies and legal uncertainties can complicate corporate investments in restoration. Governments need to provide clear incentives and frameworks to encourage corporate participation.
10.   **Alignment of Goals** – Businesses, governments, and NGOs may have different objectives, requiring strong governance structures to ensure effective collaboration.

Ensuring Long-Term Impact and Accountability

Ensuring the long-term impact and accountability of restoration financing is essential for maintaining environmental, social, and financial sustainability. While corporate, philanthropic, and market-based investments provide much-needed capital for ecosystem restoration, the success of these projects depends on transparent governance, clear monitoring frameworks, and sustained financial commitments. Effective accountability mechanisms ensure that restoration initiatives achieve their intended outcomes and continue delivering benefits over time.

Monitoring and Measuring Environmental Outcomes

Long-term restoration success requires robust monitoring systems that track ecological progress and assess the impact of investments. Key performance indicators (KPIs) for measuring environmental impact include:

- **Biodiversity Recovery** – Tracking species populations, habitat restoration progress, and ecosystem connectivity to ensure ecological resilience.
- **Carbon Sequestration and Climate Benefits** – Measuring carbon absorption rates in reforested areas and assessing climate adaptation benefits.
- **Water Quality and Soil Health** – Monitoring improvements in water filtration, soil fertility, and erosion control to evaluate restoration effectiveness.
- **Land Productivity and Community Benefits** – Assessing the socioeconomic impact of restoration, including benefits for local communities, sustainable livelihoods, and resource availability.

Independent third-party verification and standardized reporting frameworks, such as the TNFD and the GIIN, help enhance transparency and comparability across restoration projects.

Strengthening Governance and Accountability Mechanisms

Accountability in restoration finance requires strong governance structures that define clear roles, responsibilities, and oversight processes. Strategies to improve governance include:

- **Stakeholder Engagement** – Involving local communities, governments, and NGOs in project planning and implementation to ensure alignment with long-term sustainability goals.
- **Transparent Financial Reporting** – Requiring detailed disclosures on how restoration funds are allocated and spent to prevent mismanagement and greenwashing.
- **Regulatory Compliance** – Aligning projects with environmental policies, legal requirements, and sustainability standards to maintain credibility and effectiveness.

Ensuring Long-Term Financial Sustainability

Restoration efforts must secure stable funding to maintain impact beyond initial investments. Strategies for long-term financial sustainability include:

- **Blended Finance Models** – Combining public, private, and philanthropic funding to create diversified revenue streams.
- **Performance-Based Financing** – Tying funding to measurable environmental and social outcomes to encourage accountability.
- **Reinvestment Strategies** – Using revenues from carbon markets, biodiversity credits, and eco-tourism to sustain restoration projects.

Conclusion

Corporate and philanthropic investment in ecosystem restoration plays a crucial role in closing the funding gap and driving large-scale environmental recovery. As sustainability becomes an integral part of corporate strategy, businesses are increasingly directing funds toward nature-based solutions, aligning financial commitments with

ESG goals. Philanthropic foundations and environmental endowments also provide essential funding for restoration initiatives, ensuring long-term financial support for conservation efforts.

Corporate investment in restoration is often driven by regulatory requirements, stakeholder expectations, and reputational benefits. Many businesses integrate ecosystem restoration into their sustainability strategies through direct funding, corporate partnerships, and participation in carbon and biodiversity markets. Companies also engage in supply chain sustainability initiatives, ensuring that sourcing practices contribute to habitat conservation and ecosystem resilience. These corporate commitments not only support restoration efforts but also help businesses manage environmental risks and enhance long-term operational stability.

Philanthropic foundations and environmental endowments complement corporate investment by providing flexible, long-term funding that supports innovative restoration projects and community-based conservation initiatives. Unlike market-driven financial instruments, philanthropic funding is often less constrained by short-term financial returns, allowing for greater experimentation and long-term impact. Collaborative funding models, where corporations and foundations co-finance restoration projects, further enhance financial sustainability and scale.

Despite the growing role of corporate and philanthropic investment in restoration, challenges remain in ensuring transparency, accountability, and long-term commitment. Companies must go beyond one-time contributions and integrate restoration into broader business strategies, while philanthropic organizations should align funding with measurable environmental outcomes. Strengthening governance frameworks, standardizing impact reporting, and fostering multi-stakeholder collaboration will be essential for maximizing the effectiveness of corporate and philanthropic contributions to restoration finance.

As the demand for sustainable investment grows, corporate and philanthropic funding will continue to be a critical component of restoration finance. By integrating restoration into business and philanthropy, stakeholders can contribute to global conservation efforts while ensuring financial and environmental resilience.

Chapter 7: Technological Innovations in Financing Ecosystem Restoration

Technological advancements are transforming the way ecosystem restoration projects are financed, monitored, and managed. Digital tools, data analytics, and financial technologies (fintech) are enhancing transparency, efficiency, and scalability in restoration finance, attracting greater investment and improving impact measurement. Innovations such as blockchain, artificial intelligence (AI), remote sensing, and geospatial data are enabling more precise tracking of ecological outcomes, reducing financial risks, and ensuring accountability in restoration funding.

Technology is also revolutionizing market-based financial mechanisms, such as carbon credit trading, biodiversity offsets, and PES. Digital platforms facilitate real-time transactions, automate reporting, and enhance accessibility for investors, making it easier to scale up restoration finance.

This chapter explores key technological innovations in financing restoration, their role in improving investment efficiency, and the challenges and opportunities associated with their implementation. By leveraging technology, restoration finance can become more transparent, efficient, and impactful, supporting global efforts to restore degraded ecosystems.

Emerging Fintech Solutions (AI, Blockchain, Big Data)

Financial technology (fintech) is playing an increasingly important role in ecosystem restoration by improving transparency, efficiency, and scalability in funding mechanisms. Emerging technologies such as AI, blockchain, and big data analytics are transforming restoration finance by streamlining investment processes, reducing financial risks, and enhancing the tracking of environmental outcomes. These innovations help attract more capital to restoration projects by increasing investor confidence and ensuring measurable ecological impact.

AI in Restoration Finance

AI is revolutionizing financial decision-making and risk assessment in restoration projects by analyzing large datasets to identify investment opportunities, predict environmental outcomes, and optimize funding allocation.

- **Risk Assessment and Investment Optimization** – AI-driven models assess financial and environmental risks, helping investors make data-driven decisions. By analyzing factors such as climate patterns, deforestation rates, and land degradation, AI improves the accuracy of financial projections for restoration projects.
- **Automated Monitoring and Impact Measurement** – AI-powered satellite imagery and remote sensing technologies track ecological restoration progress in real time. These tools detect changes in forest cover, water quality, and biodiversity, ensuring that restoration investments deliver measurable environmental benefits.
- **Predictive Analytics for Ecosystem Services** – AI helps estimate the long-term benefits of restoration projects, such as carbon sequestration potential, water purification efficiency, and soil regeneration capacity, providing investors with clearer insights into expected returns.

Blockchain for Transparency and Accountability

Blockchain technology is improving the transparency, security, and accountability of financial transactions in ecosystem restoration. By creating decentralized and tamper-proof records, blockchain ensures that funds are used as intended and that environmental impacts are verifiable.

16.   **Transparent Funding Allocation** – Blockchain-based smart contracts automate financial transactions and ensure that funds are disbursed only when predefined environmental milestones are met. This reduces fraud and mismanagement in restoration financing.

17.   **Carbon Credit and Biodiversity Tokenization** – Blockchain enables the creation and trading of digital assets, such as tokenized carbon credits and biodiversity credits. These digital tokens represent verified ecological benefits and can be bought and sold on decentralized platforms, enhancing the liquidity of restoration finance.

18.   **Decentralized Impact Verification** – Blockchain-powered platforms facilitate third-party verification of restoration outcomes, ensuring that project claims align with actual environmental improvements. This enhances investor trust and attracts more private capital to restoration efforts.

Big Data and Analytics in Restoration Finance

Big data analytics enhances decision-making in restoration finance by aggregating and analyzing vast amounts of ecological, financial, and social data. These insights help investors, policymakers, and conservation organizations design more effective and scalable restoration strategies.

- **Real-Time Environmental Monitoring** – Big data systems integrate satellite imagery, IoT (Internet of Things) sensors, and climate models to provide real-time insights into ecosystem changes. This improves the ability to track deforestation, land degradation, and habitat restoration progress.
- **Market Intelligence for Sustainable Investments** – Data-driven platforms analyze trends in carbon markets, biodiversity credits, and restoration-related financial instruments. This helps investors identify high-impact opportunities and assess market risks.
- **Social and Economic Impact Assessment** – Big data tools evaluate how restoration projects affect local communities,

tracking factors such as employment generation, water access, and agricultural productivity. These insights support more inclusive and equitable restoration financing strategies.

Challenges and Opportunities

While fintech solutions offer significant benefits for restoration finance, challenges remain in terms of adoption, scalability, and regulatory frameworks.

- **Data Standardization and Interoperability** – Ensuring compatibility between different data sources and platforms is essential for maximizing the effectiveness of AI, blockchain, and big data applications.
- **Regulatory and Policy Uncertainty** – Governments and financial institutions must establish clear regulatory frameworks to facilitate the integration of fintech solutions into restoration finance.
- **Technical Capacity and Infrastructure** – Widespread adoption of fintech solutions requires investment in digital infrastructure, particularly in regions with limited technological access.

Despite these challenges, emerging fintech solutions have the potential to revolutionize restoration finance by improving transparency, efficiency, and impact measurement. As technology continues to evolve, AI, blockchain, and big data will play an increasingly critical role in mobilizing capital for large-scale ecosystem restoration efforts.

Digital Tokens and Biodiversity Credits

Digital tokens and biodiversity credits are emerging financial mechanisms that leverage technology to enhance transparency, efficiency, and scalability in ecosystem restoration finance. These tools provide measurable financial incentives for biodiversity conservation, allowing investors, corporations, and governments to support restoration projects while ensuring accountability and impact verification. By integrating blockchain and digital asset technologies, biodiversity credits and tokenized environmental assets create new opportunities for funding nature-based solutions.

Understanding Biodiversity Credits

Biodiversity credits function similarly to carbon credits but focus on conserving and restoring ecosystems rather than reducing greenhouse gas emissions. These credits represent measurable environmental improvements, such as habitat restoration, species protection, and ecosystem enhancement. They allow businesses and investors to offset biodiversity loss or demonstrate their commitment to sustainability.

- **Voluntary Biodiversity Credits** – Companies and organizations purchase biodiversity credits to compensate for their environmental impact, aligning with corporate sustainability goals and regulatory frameworks.
- **Regulated Biodiversity Offsets** – Some governments mandate biodiversity offsets, requiring developers to compensate for habitat destruction by purchasing credits that fund restoration projects.

Digital Tokens in Restoration Finance

Digital tokens are blockchain-based assets that represent ownership, funding contributions, or verified ecological benefits. Tokenization enables the efficient trading, tracking, and monetization of restoration investments, enhancing the liquidity and accessibility of biodiversity finance.

- **Nature-Based Tokens** – Digital tokens can represent specific ecosystem services, such as forest preservation, wetland restoration, or species conservation, allowing investors to support targeted restoration initiatives.

- **Carbon and Biodiversity Token Integration** – Some platforms integrate biodiversity credits with carbon markets, enabling investors to purchase digital assets that deliver both carbon sequestration and ecological benefits.

Advantages of Digital Tokens and Biodiversity Credits

- **Enhanced Transparency and Verification** – Blockchain technology ensures that biodiversity credits and digital tokens are linked to verifiable restoration outcomes, reducing fraud and greenwashing concerns.
- **Scalability and Accessibility** – Digital platforms enable global participation, allowing businesses and individuals to invest in restoration projects from anywhere in the world.
- **Market Liquidity** – Tokenized biodiversity assets create tradeable financial instruments, improving access to funding for conservation initiatives.

Challenges and Considerations

Despite their potential, biodiversity credits and digital tokens face challenges related to standardization, regulatory frameworks, and adoption. Establishing clear verification protocols and governance structures is essential for ensuring credibility and long-term success.

Crowdfunding and Community-Based Financing

Crowdfunding and community-based financing are innovative approaches that mobilize financial resources for ecosystem restoration by engaging individuals, local communities, and small-scale investors. These models provide an alternative to traditional funding mechanisms, allowing restoration projects to secure capital from a broad base of contributors. By leveraging digital platforms and grassroots networks, crowdfunding and community-based financing enhance public participation in conservation efforts and create inclusive opportunities for sustainable investment.

Understanding Crowdfunding for Restoration

Crowdfunding is a financing model that raises small amounts of money from a large number of people, typically through online platforms. It has gained traction as an effective tool for supporting environmental projects, including reforestation, habitat restoration, and biodiversity conservation. Crowdfunding allows individuals and organizations to contribute directly to specific restoration initiatives, often in exchange for symbolic rewards, project updates, or impact reports.

There are several types of crowdfunding relevant to ecosystem restoration:

13. **Donation-Based Crowdfunding** – Supporters contribute funds without expecting financial returns. This model is commonly used by environmental NGOs and conservation groups to raise money for restoration projects.
14. **Reward-Based Crowdfunding** – Contributors receive non-financial rewards, such as tree-planting certificates, personalized project updates, or eco-friendly merchandise, in exchange for their support.
15. **Equity Crowdfunding** – Investors receive ownership stakes in conservation-focused enterprises, such as sustainable forestry initiatives or eco-tourism ventures.
16. **Debt Crowdfunding (Peer-to-Peer Lending)** – Individuals or organizations lend money to restoration projects with the expectation of repayment over time, sometimes with interest.

Crowdfunding platforms such as GoFundMe, Kickstarter, and specialized environmental crowdfunding sites like EarthEnable and Trine provide accessible channels for raising funds and engaging public interest in restoration efforts.

Community-Based Financing for Restoration

Community-based financing involves local stakeholders directly in the funding and management of restoration initiatives. These models empower communities to take ownership of conservation projects, ensuring long-term sustainability and local engagement.

Key community-based financing mechanisms include:

12. **Cooperative Investment Models** – Local communities form cooperatives to pool resources for sustainable land management, agroforestry, or habitat restoration. Members contribute financially and share the benefits of restored ecosystems.
13. **Community Conservation Funds** – These funds collect financial contributions from local businesses, residents, and government agencies to support ongoing restoration efforts, ensuring stable, long-term financing.
14. **Microfinance and Social Lending** – Small loans are provided to farmers, landowners, and entrepreneurs for eco-friendly businesses that promote landscape restoration and biodiversity conservation.
15. **PES Programs** – Community members receive compensation for restoring or maintaining ecosystems that provide valuable services such as water purification, carbon sequestration, and soil stabilization.

Advantages of Crowdfunding and Community-Based Financing

These models offer several benefits for ecosystem restoration:

11. **Inclusivity and Public Engagement** – Crowdfunding and community financing democratize restoration funding, allowing individuals and small investors to contribute to environmental sustainability.
12. **Flexibility and Scalability** – These models provide adaptable financing structures that can support projects of varying sizes, from small local initiatives to large-scale restoration efforts.

13.   **Local Empowerment and Ownership** –
Community-based financing ensures that restoration projects
align with local needs and priorities, fostering long-term
commitment to environmental stewardship.
14.   **Diversification of Funding Sources** – By
complementing traditional finance mechanisms,
crowdfunding and community financing reduce reliance on
government or corporate funding, making restoration efforts
more resilient.

Challenges and Considerations

Despite their potential, crowdfunding and community-based
financing face several challenges:

- **Limited Funding Capacity** – Compared to institutional
  investors, crowdfunding and community financing generate
  smaller amounts of capital, requiring projects to secure
  additional funding sources.
- **Donor Fatigue and Market Competition** – Crowdfunding
  campaigns must continuously engage supporters and compete
  for attention among numerous social and environmental
  causes.
- **Project Transparency and Accountability** – Ensuring that
  funds are used effectively and that restoration outcomes are
  verifiable is crucial for maintaining donor trust.
- **Regulatory and Administrative Barriers** – Navigating
  legal and financial regulations for community-led investment
  models can be complex and time-consuming.

Monitoring and Transparency in Restoration Finance

Ensuring effective monitoring and transparency in restoration
finance is essential for maintaining investor confidence, securing
long-term funding, and achieving measurable environmental
outcomes. As ecosystem restoration projects attract increasing levels
of public, private, and philanthropic investment, robust tracking

mechanisms and clear reporting standards are needed to verify the impact of financial flows and ensure accountability.

Importance of Monitoring in Restoration Finance

Monitoring allows stakeholders to assess the progress and effectiveness of restoration initiatives, ensuring that funds are used as intended and delivering tangible ecological benefits. Key objectives of monitoring in restoration finance include:

- **Tracking Financial Allocation** – Ensuring that funds are directed toward restoration activities rather than administrative inefficiencies or unrelated expenditures.
- **Assessing Environmental Impact** – Measuring improvements in biodiversity, carbon sequestration, soil health, and water quality to confirm that restoration projects achieve their intended goals.
- **Ensuring Compliance with Standards** – Aligning projects with international sustainability frameworks such as the TNFD, Global Reporting Initiative (GRI), and Science-Based Targets for Nature (SBTN) to maintain credibility and consistency in reporting.

Technological Innovations for Transparency

Advancements in financial technology and digital monitoring tools have improved transparency in restoration finance, making it easier to track investments and assess impact in real time. Key innovations include:

- **Blockchain for Secure Transactions** – Blockchain technology enables transparent and tamper-proof financial records, ensuring that restoration funds are allocated and used as intended.
- **Satellite Imaging and Remote Sensing** – High-resolution satellite data helps monitor deforestation, reforestation, and

land degradation, providing objective evidence of restoration progress.
- **AI and Big Data Analytics** – Machine learning algorithms analyze large datasets to detect trends, predict ecological outcomes, and optimize resource allocation in restoration projects.

Challenges and Considerations

Despite technological advancements, challenges remain in achieving full transparency in restoration finance:

- **Standardization of Metrics** – Variability in restoration methodologies makes it difficult to develop universal impact measurement standards.
- **Verification Costs** – Independent audits and third-party impact assessments require financial resources that may not be available for smaller projects.
- **Data Accessibility** – Ensuring open access to financial and environmental data while maintaining privacy and regulatory compliance remains a challenge.

Conclusion

Technological innovations are transforming the landscape of restoration finance by enhancing transparency, efficiency, and accountability in investment processes. As ecosystem restoration projects scale up, emerging technologies such as blockchain, AI, and big data analytics are playing a crucial role in improving financial flows, impact measurement, and stakeholder trust. By leveraging these advancements, restoration finance can become more accessible, data-driven, and results-oriented.

Blockchain technology enhances financial transparency by creating tamper-proof records of transactions, ensuring that funds are allocated appropriately and that environmental outcomes are verifiable. Smart contracts further streamline funding mechanisms by automating payments based on project milestones, reducing inefficiencies and minimizing risks of fund mismanagement. These innovations improve investor confidence and encourage greater participation in restoration finance.

AI and big data analytics contribute to more accurate risk assessments, project evaluations, and environmental monitoring. AI-powered predictive models help investors assess the long-term viability of restoration projects by analyzing climate trends, land use changes, and ecosystem health indicators. Remote sensing and satellite imaging provide real-time data on deforestation, biodiversity loss, and habitat restoration progress, enabling better decision-making and impact verification.

Digital tokens and biodiversity credits offer new financial instruments that integrate restoration efforts into broader economic systems. Tokenization of ecosystem services allows investors and businesses to participate in conservation finance through tradable digital assets, creating additional funding streams for restoration initiatives. Crowdfunding platforms and decentralized finance (DeFi) models further expand access to restoration funding by enabling small-scale investors and communities to contribute to conservation efforts.

Despite their potential, technological innovations in restoration finance require standardized regulations, clear governance frameworks, and widespread adoption to maximize impact. Ensuring interoperability between financial and environmental data systems, enhancing cybersecurity protections, and promoting cross-sector collaboration will be key to advancing these solutions.

As digital finance and environmental monitoring technologies continue to evolve, they will play an increasingly vital role in scaling up restoration finance. By integrating technology with financial mechanisms, stakeholders can enhance the efficiency, accountability, and accessibility of restoration investments, ensuring long-term sustainability and resilience.

Chapter 8: Risk Management and Governance in Ecosystem Restoration Finance

Effective risk management and governance are essential for ensuring the long-term success of ecosystem restoration finance. As restoration projects involve multiple stakeholders, diverse financial instruments, and complex ecological factors, strong governance frameworks and risk mitigation strategies are required to maintain financial stability, environmental integrity, and investor confidence.

Restoration finance faces risks such as uncertain financial returns, regulatory changes, environmental unpredictability, and project implementation challenges. Addressing these risks requires clear policies, standardized reporting, transparent financial management, and multi-stakeholder collaboration. Governance structures must also ensure accountability, prevent misallocation of funds, and align restoration investments with global sustainability goals.

This chapter explores key risk management strategies, governance frameworks, and best practices for maintaining transparency and financial integrity in restoration finance. By implementing effective governance mechanisms and mitigating financial and environmental risks, restoration initiatives can achieve long-term sustainability and attract continued investment.

Financial Risks and Mitigation Strategies

Ecosystem restoration finance involves various financial risks that can impact the feasibility, sustainability, and attractiveness of restoration investments. These risks arise from market fluctuations, regulatory uncertainties, environmental unpredictability, and project implementation challenges. Addressing these financial risks through mitigation strategies is essential to ensure long-term project viability, investor confidence, and the achievement of restoration goals.

Key Financial Risks in Restoration Finance

1. Market and Investment Risks

- o Restoration finance often depends on emerging financial instruments, such as green bonds, biodiversity credits, and carbon markets. Market volatility can affect the value of these assets and influence investor confidence.
- o Fluctuations in demand for ecosystem services, such as carbon sequestration or water purification, may impact financial returns.
- o Limited liquidity in restoration-related financial instruments may deter institutional investors looking for more stable and tradable assets.

2. Regulatory and Policy Risks

- o Shifts in environmental regulations, tax policies, or subsidy programs can alter the financial landscape for restoration projects.
- o Inconsistent or unclear legal frameworks may create uncertainty for investors and project developers.
- o Changes in government priorities or political instability can affect public-sector funding and incentives for restoration.

3. Project Implementation and Operational Risks

- o Delays in project execution due to technical challenges, land disputes, or logistical constraints can lead to cost overruns.
- o Inadequate governance structures may result in mismanagement of funds, reducing project efficiency and impact.
- o Stakeholder conflicts, especially in community-led restoration initiatives, can slow down progress and increase costs.

4. Environmental and Climate Risks

- o Climate variability, natural disasters, and ecological uncertainties may impact restoration success, reducing expected financial returns.
- o Unforeseen environmental changes, such as prolonged droughts or invasive species, may require additional investment to adapt restoration efforts.

Mitigation Strategies for Financial Risks

19. Diversification of Revenue Streams

- a. Combining multiple funding sources, including public grants, private investments, carbon markets, and biodiversity credits, can reduce reliance on a single revenue stream.
- b. Exploring innovative financial instruments such as sustainability-linked bonds or blended finance models can enhance financial resilience.

Regulatory Risk Management

- Engaging with policymakers and aligning restoration finance with global environmental agreements, such as the Paris Agreement and the Convention on Biological Diversity, can ensure long-term regulatory stability.
- Legal due diligence and compliance assessments help identify and address potential policy-related risks before project implementation.

Robust Financial Planning and Risk Assessment

- Developing comprehensive financial models that account for risk scenarios, cost projections, and contingency plans can improve investment security.
- Conducting risk assessments to evaluate potential threats and develop mitigation strategies ensures better preparedness for financial uncertainties.

- **Insurance and Risk-Sharing Mechanisms**

  - Climate risk insurance can protect against environmental uncertainties, such as extreme weather events that may impact restoration outcomes.
  - PPPs and co-financing arrangements distribute financial risks among multiple stakeholders, reducing exposure for individual investors.

- **Transparent Governance and Impact Monitoring**

  - Establishing clear governance structures with defined financial accountability mechanisms enhances investor confidence.
  - Regular impact assessments and financial audits improve transparency and ensure that funds are being used efficiently and effectively.

Regulatory Frameworks and Global Governance

Effective regulatory frameworks and global governance play a critical role in shaping restoration finance by providing clear policies, standards, and accountability mechanisms. As ecosystem restoration gains prominence in global sustainability agendas, well-defined regulations and governance structures ensure financial transparency, protect investments, and align restoration efforts with international environmental goals. Strong regulatory frameworks also encourage private sector participation, enhance investor confidence, and create financial incentives for large-scale restoration initiatives.

Key Regulatory Frameworks Supporting Restoration Finance

Several international and national regulatory frameworks influence the financing of ecosystem restoration:

- **Paris Agreement (2015)**

- o A legally binding international treaty that sets climate action targets, including commitments to land restoration and nature-based solutions.
- o Encourages carbon markets, climate finance mechanisms, and investments in reforestation and sustainable land management.

- **Convention on Biological Diversity (CBD) and Kunming-Montreal Global Biodiversity Framework**

  - o Establishes global biodiversity conservation targets, including commitments to restore at least 30% of degraded ecosystems by 2030.
  - o Promotes biodiversity credits, financial incentives, and corporate accountability in conservation finance.

- **UN SDGs**

  - o Goal 15 (Life on Land) and Goal 13 (Climate Action) emphasize sustainable land use, forest restoration, and ecosystem conservation.
  - o Encourages governments and financial institutions to integrate restoration into sustainable development policies.

- **EU Green Deal and Sustainable Finance Taxonomy**

  - o The EU Sustainable Finance Taxonomy classifies environmentally sustainable investments, ensuring that restoration finance aligns with measurable sustainability objectives.
  - o Green bonds and sustainability-linked finance are regulated under the EU Green Bond Standard, promoting transparency and impact reporting.

- **TNFD**

- o Provides voluntary guidelines for corporations and financial institutions to assess and disclose nature-related risks and opportunities.
- o Helps align private sector investments with biodiversity and ecosystem restoration goals.

Governance Structures for Restoration Finance

Global governance structures ensure coordination among governments, financial institutions, and private sector actors in ecosystem restoration. Key governance mechanisms include:

17. **Multilateral Financial Institutions** – Organizations such as the World Bank, GCF, and GEF provide financial support, technical assistance, and policy guidance for restoration projects worldwide.
18. **PPPs** – Collaborative models between governments, corporations, and NGOs facilitate restoration financing by combining public grants with private sector investment.
19. **Carbon and Biodiversity Markets** – International carbon markets, such as the United Nations Clean Development Mechanism (CDM) and voluntary biodiversity credit markets, provide financial incentives for restoration through tradable environmental assets.

Challenges in Regulatory Compliance and Global Governance

Despite progress, regulatory frameworks and governance structures face several challenges:

16. **Fragmented Policies** – Different regulatory approaches across countries create inconsistencies, making it difficult to establish unified financial mechanisms for restoration.
17. **Lack of Enforcement** – Many restoration commitments remain voluntary, limiting accountability and long-term financial sustainability.

18. **Complexity of Financial Regulations** – Investors and project developers often struggle to navigate complex regulatory requirements, leading to delays in funding allocation.

Opportunities for Strengthening Governance

15. **Harmonizing International Standards** – Establishing global guidelines for restoration finance, such as standardized biodiversity credit certification, can enhance regulatory consistency.
16. **Enhancing Transparency and Reporting** – Strengthening environmental impact disclosures and financial reporting ensures accountability in restoration investments.
17. **Integrating Nature-Based Solutions into Climate Finance** – Aligning restoration finance with climate adaptation and mitigation funding can expand investment opportunities.

Transparency and Stakeholder Engagement

Transparency and stakeholder engagement are critical components of effective restoration finance, ensuring accountability, trust, and long-term success in ecosystem restoration projects. As financial mechanisms for restoration become more complex, clear reporting frameworks, open communication, and inclusive stakeholder participation are necessary to build investor confidence, align interests, and drive meaningful environmental impact. By integrating transparency and engagement into restoration finance, projects can attract sustainable investment, mitigate risks, and foster long-term support from communities, governments, and private sector actors.

The Role of Transparency in Restoration Finance

Transparency in restoration finance refers to the clear and accessible disclosure of financial flows, project outcomes, and impact assessments. It ensures that investments in restoration projects are allocated effectively and that environmental benefits are measurable and verifiable. Key aspects of financial transparency include:

- **Clear Financial Reporting** – Investors and stakeholders require detailed reports on how funds are allocated, spent, and monitored to ensure accountability and prevent mismanagement.
- **Standardized Impact Measurement** – Using globally recognized frameworks such as the TNFD and the GIIN improves the credibility of financial reporting and impact assessments.
- **Third-Party Verification** – Independent audits and external evaluations enhance trust by validating financial transactions, ecological progress, and compliance with sustainability standards.
- **Accessible Data and Open Reporting** – Publicly available financial and environmental performance data enable informed decision-making and reduce the risks of greenwashing.

Importance of Stakeholder Engagement in Restoration Finance

Ecosystem restoration projects involve multiple stakeholders, including governments, financial institutions, corporations, NGOs, local communities, and indigenous groups. Meaningful engagement ensures that restoration initiatives align with environmental goals, social needs, and economic priorities. Key benefits of stakeholder engagement include:

- **Aligning Interests and Expectations** – Collaborative decision-making ensures that investors, governments, and local communities share common goals and responsibilities.
- **Enhancing Social Acceptance** – Projects that involve local communities in planning and implementation are more likely to succeed, as they incorporate traditional knowledge and address local concerns.

- **Ensuring Long-Term Sustainability** – Engaged stakeholders are more likely to support restoration projects beyond initial funding phases, contributing to long-term ecosystem resilience.
- **Mitigating Conflict and Risk** – Transparent communication and participatory governance help prevent disputes over land use, resource allocation, and project implementation.

Mechanisms for Enhancing Transparency and Engagement

Several mechanisms can improve transparency and stakeholder engagement in restoration finance:

- **Multi-Stakeholder Platforms** – Initiatives such as the UN Environment Programme Finance Initiative (UNEP FI) provide forums for financial institutions, businesses, and policymakers to collaborate on sustainable finance strategies.
- **PPPs** – These partnerships integrate public funding with private sector investment, ensuring financial oversight and broader accountability.
- **Community-Based Monitoring Systems** – Engaging local communities in data collection, land management, and ecological monitoring ensures inclusive participation and long-term ownership.
- **Technology-Driven Transparency** – Blockchain, satellite imagery, and AI-driven data analytics improve monitoring and verification, ensuring that restoration finance delivers measurable results.

Challenges in Achieving Transparency and Stakeholder Engagement

Despite progress, several challenges hinder full transparency and effective engagement in restoration finance:

- **Data Standardization and Reporting Complexity** – Differences in financial and environmental reporting systems make it difficult to compare project outcomes across regions and institutions.

- **Ensuring Meaningful Participation** – Some projects involve stakeholders superficially, rather than actively incorporating their input into decision-making.
- **Managing Conflicting Interests** – Restoration finance often requires balancing environmental objectives with economic and social priorities, leading to conflicts between stakeholders.

Ensuring Long-Term Financial Viability

Long-term financial viability is essential for sustaining ecosystem restoration efforts beyond initial funding phases. While short-term grants and philanthropic donations provide critical early-stage support, restoration projects require stable, recurring financial resources to maintain ecological gains, adapt to changing environmental conditions, and scale impact over time. To achieve financial sustainability, restoration initiatives must integrate diversified funding sources, leverage market-based mechanisms, and develop innovative financial structures that align conservation goals with economic incentives.

Strategies for Long-Term Financial Viability

- **Diversifying Funding Sources**

    o Relying on a single source of funding can lead to financial instability. A combination of public funding, private sector investment, carbon markets, biodiversity credits, and sustainable debt instruments enhances resilience and reduces reliance on unpredictable financial flows.
    o Blended finance models, which combine concessional capital from governments or development banks with private investment, help mitigate risks and attract long-term investors.

- **Market-Based Financial Mechanisms**

  o **Carbon and Biodiversity Markets** – Generating revenue through the sale of carbon credits, biodiversity offsets, and nature-based solutions allows restoration projects to integrate into existing financial systems, ensuring long-term income.
  o **PES** – These schemes compensate landowners, farmers, and businesses for protecting and restoring ecosystems that provide essential services such as clean water, carbon sequestration, and soil stability.

- **Performance-Based Financing Models**

  o **Sustainability-Linked Bonds and Loans** – Financial instruments that tie investment terms to environmental performance metrics encourage long-term ecological and financial sustainability.
  o **Impact Investment Funds** – Attracting investors who seek both financial returns and positive environmental outcomes ensures continued capital flow into restoration projects.

- **PPPs and Community Engagement**

  o PPP models leverage both public and private sector expertise and funding to share risks and create sustainable financing structures.
  o Community-based financing initiatives involve local stakeholders in funding and governance, ensuring long-term commitment to restoration success.

- **Endowment and Trust Funds**

  Establishing environmental endowments and conservation trust funds provides permanent financial support for restoration, with investment returns funding long-term ecosystem management and maintenance.

Conclusion

Risk management and governance are essential for ensuring the effectiveness, transparency, and long-term sustainability of restoration finance. As ecosystem restoration projects attract increasing levels of public and private investment, robust governance frameworks and risk mitigation strategies are required to manage financial, environmental, and regulatory uncertainties. Without strong oversight and accountability measures, restoration finance may face inefficiencies, misallocation of funds, and challenges in achieving measurable ecological outcomes.

Financial risks, including market volatility, uncertain returns, and regulatory changes, can deter investment in restoration projects. Addressing these risks requires diversified funding models, performance-based financial instruments, and risk-sharing mechanisms such as blended finance and PPPs. Additionally, insurance products like parametric climate insurance can protect restoration investments from environmental shocks, ensuring financial stability over the long term.

Governance frameworks play a critical role in maintaining investor confidence and ensuring financial transparency. Standardized impact measurement, third-party verification, and adherence to global sustainability frameworks—such as the TNFD and the GIIN—help establish credibility in restoration finance. Clear regulatory policies and legal safeguards also prevent greenwashing and ensure that financial commitments translate into tangible environmental benefits.

Stakeholder engagement is another key component of strong governance in restoration finance. Multi-stakeholder collaboration, including governments, financial institutions, corporations, NGOs, and local communities, ensures that restoration projects align with both environmental and social priorities. Inclusive decision-making and participatory governance models enhance accountability and contribute to long-term project success.

Despite progress in strengthening risk management and governance structures, challenges remain in standardizing financial reporting, integrating restoration finance into mainstream investment portfolios, and ensuring long-term commitment from stakeholders. Addressing these challenges will require ongoing policy development, technological innovation, and knowledge sharing across sectors.

As restoration finance continues to evolve, implementing effective risk management strategies and governance frameworks will be essential for scaling up investment, minimizing financial and environmental risks, and ensuring that restoration initiatives deliver meaningful and lasting impact.

Chapter 9: Scaling Up Sustainable Finance for Global Ecosystem Restoration

Achieving large-scale ecosystem restoration requires significant financial resources, innovative investment mechanisms, and strong multi-sector collaboration. While sustainable finance has gained traction in supporting restoration projects, the challenge remains in mobilizing capital at the scale necessary to meet global restoration targets. Expanding financial instruments, improving regulatory frameworks, and integrating restoration finance into mainstream investment strategies are essential for driving long-term impact.

This chapter explores strategies for scaling up sustainable finance for global ecosystem restoration, including strengthening public-private partnerships, increasing investment in market-based solutions, and enhancing international financial cooperation. It also examines the role of financial innovation, technology, and policy alignment in accelerating funding for restoration initiatives. By addressing key barriers and leveraging financial opportunities, restoration finance can transition from niche investments to a global movement that supports environmental resilience and long-term sustainability.

Opportunities for Financial Innovation in Restoration

Financial innovation is playing a critical role in scaling up ecosystem restoration by developing new investment models, improving capital efficiency, and creating market-driven solutions for sustainable finance. As the demand for restoration finance grows, innovative financial instruments and mechanisms are essential to attract investment, reduce financial risks, and integrate restoration efforts into mainstream economic systems. By leveraging technology, market-based approaches, and public-private collaboration, financial innovation can unlock new funding streams and accelerate large-scale restoration initiatives.

Key Financial Innovations in Restoration Finance

- **Sustainability-Linked Bonds and Loans**

    o Unlike traditional green bonds, SLBs and sustainability-linked loans (SLLs) tie financial terms to environmental performance indicators. Companies or governments issuing these bonds commit to achieving specific restoration goals, such as reforesting degraded land or improving biodiversity conservation.
    o If targets are met, issuers benefit from lower interest rates or financial incentives, encouraging long-term investment in restoration projects.

- **Carbon and Biodiversity Markets**

    o Carbon credit trading has evolved as a major financial mechanism supporting reforestation and afforestation projects. Companies purchase carbon credits to offset their emissions, providing direct funding for ecosystem restoration.
    o Biodiversity credits function similarly, allowing businesses to invest in conservation programs to compensate for habitat loss and ecosystem degradation. Standardized biodiversity credit markets can help scale up restoration finance while ensuring environmental accountability.

- **Debt-for-Nature Swaps and Sovereign Green Bonds**

    o Debt-for-nature swaps enable developing countries to restructure debt obligations in exchange for commitments to environmental conservation and restoration. By directing funds toward ecosystem recovery, these agreements enhance financial stability while preserving natural resources.
    o Sovereign green bonds, issued by governments, raise capital specifically for nature-based solutions, including land restoration, watershed management,

and sustainable forestry. These bonds align national economic policies with environmental goals.

20.   **Blended Finance Models**

    a. Blended finance combines public, private, and philanthropic capital to de-risk restoration investments and attract private sector participation.
    b. Impact investment funds and PPPs use concessional funding from governments or development banks to reduce financial risks, encouraging large-scale commercial investment in restoration projects.

21.   **Digital Tokens and Blockchain-Based Financing**

    a. Tokenization of ecosystem services allows restoration projects to issue digital assets linked to environmental benefits, such as carbon sequestration or biodiversity conservation. Investors can trade or hold these tokens, creating new financial incentives for sustainable land management.
    b. Blockchain technology ensures transparency in financial transactions, reducing risks of greenwashing and improving accountability in restoration finance.

22.   **Insurance and Risk Mitigation Instruments**

    a. Parametric insurance for restoration projects provides financial protection against climate-related disasters, such as wildfires, floods, and droughts. These policies automatically trigger payouts when predefined environmental conditions occur, ensuring funding continuity for restoration efforts.
    b. Resilience bonds and nature-based insurance solutions help businesses and communities invest in restoration as a means of climate adaptation and risk reduction.

Challenges and Considerations

Despite its potential, financial innovation in restoration faces challenges that must be addressed to maximize impact:

- **Standardization and Regulation** – New financial instruments require clear regulations and verification standards to prevent misuse and ensure transparency.
- **Market Development and Liquidity** – Many restoration-focused financial products, such as biodiversity credits, remain in early-stage development and require broader market adoption.
- **Scaling Investment to Global Levels** – While pilot projects demonstrate success, scaling financial innovations to a global level requires stronger financial infrastructure, investor confidence, and policy support.

Strengthening Multi-Stakeholder Collaboration

Multi-stakeholder collaboration is essential for scaling up sustainable finance for ecosystem restoration. Effective restoration finance requires the combined efforts of governments, private sector investors, NGOs, multilateral institutions, and local communities. By fostering collaboration, stakeholders can align financial resources, technical expertise, and policy frameworks to create impactful and scalable restoration initiatives. Strong partnerships ensure that restoration finance is deployed efficiently, meets long-term sustainability goals, and benefits both ecosystems and societies.

Key Stakeholders in Restoration Finance

Governments and Public Institutions

- National and local governments play a critical role in creating regulatory frameworks, providing public funding, and integrating restoration finance into broader economic and climate policies.

- Public agencies can issue sovereign green bonds, implement incentive programs, and establish environmental taxes or subsidies to attract private investment.

Private Sector and Institutional Investors

- Businesses and financial institutions contribute funding through corporate sustainability commitments, impact investing, and green financial instruments such as sustainability-linked bonds and carbon markets.
- Institutional investors, such as pension funds and asset managers, are increasingly integrating ESG criteria into investment portfolios, supporting large-scale restoration projects.

Multilateral and Development Finance Institutions

- Organizations like the World Bank, GCF, GEF, and United Nations Development Programme (UNDP) provide concessional finance, technical assistance, and policy guidance to scale up restoration efforts.
- These institutions help de-risk private investment by offering blended finance models, loan guarantees, and co-financing mechanisms.

NGOs and Conservation Groups

- NGOs facilitate restoration finance by designing and implementing projects, conducting environmental impact assessments, and ensuring accountability in financial flows.
- Conservation organizations such as The Nature Conservancy, World Wildlife Fund (WWF), and International Union for Conservation of Nature (IUCN) play a key role in connecting investors with credible restoration initiatives.

Local Communities and Indigenous Groups

20. Community-based restoration models ensure that financing mechanisms align with local needs and priorities, enhancing long-term project success.
21. Indigenous knowledge and traditional land management practices contribute valuable insights into ecosystem restoration, improving project design and implementation.

Strategies for Strengthening Multi-Stakeholder Collaboration

PPPs

19. Governments and private sector actors can co-develop restoration projects, leveraging public funds to attract corporate investment and reduce financial risks.
20. PPPs help scale up nature-based solutions by integrating restoration finance into infrastructure, agriculture, and supply chain sustainability strategies.

Multi-Stakeholder Platforms and Coalitions

18. Platforms such as the UN Environment Programme Finance Initiative (UNEP FI), Business for Nature, and Natural Capital Coalition bring together diverse stakeholders to align restoration finance with global sustainability goals.
19. Industry alliances create shared commitments, knowledge-sharing opportunities, and standardized reporting frameworks to improve financial transparency.

Collaborative Blended Finance Models

- Combining public, private, and philanthropic capital through blended finance structures ensures that restoration finance benefits from risk-sharing mechanisms and diversified investment strategies.
- Impact investment funds, revolving loan funds, and pooled conservation finance initiatives encourage multi-sector participation in restoration funding.

Technology-Enabled Collaboration

- Digital platforms, blockchain technology, and AI-driven analytics improve financial transparency and facilitate seamless collaboration between stakeholders.
- Open-access environmental data portals allow investors, policymakers, and conservation groups to track restoration progress and measure impact effectively.

Challenges in Multi-Stakeholder Collaboration

Despite its advantages, multi-stakeholder collaboration in restoration finance faces several challenges:

- **Diverging Interests and Priorities** – Governments, investors, and conservation groups may have different objectives, requiring strong governance mechanisms to align financial and ecological goals.
- **Regulatory and Policy Barriers** – Inconsistent policies across jurisdictions can complicate cross-sector partnerships and investment structures.
- **Monitoring and Accountability Issues** – Ensuring that financial contributions translate into measurable restoration outcomes requires standardized reporting and third-party verification.

Bridging Investment Gaps Through New Models

Scaling up sustainable finance for global ecosystem restoration requires bridging existing investment gaps by developing innovative funding models. While restoration projects generate long-term environmental and economic benefits, securing sufficient capital remains a challenge due to financial risks, unclear returns, and regulatory barriers. By leveraging new financial instruments, integrating public and private sector funding, and creating scalable investment models, restoration finance can become more attractive to investors while ensuring long-term sustainability.

Understanding the Investment Gap in Restoration Finance

Despite growing interest in nature-based solutions, ecosystem restoration remains significantly underfunded. The UNEP estimates that closing the global biodiversity and ecosystem restoration financing gap requires hundreds of billions of dollars annually. Key reasons for this shortfall include:

- **Perceived Financial Risks** – Restoration projects often have long payback periods and uncertain revenue streams, making them less attractive to traditional investors.
- **Limited Market Maturity** – Unlike renewable energy or carbon markets, biodiversity finance is still developing, with few standardized investment models.
- **Regulatory and Policy Uncertainty** – Inconsistent environmental policies and fragmented carbon and biodiversity credit markets create challenges in securing long-term investment.

New Models for Bridging Investment Gaps

Several innovative financial models are emerging to address these challenges and attract capital for large-scale restoration projects:

Blended Finance for De-Risking Investments

Blended finance combines public, private, and philanthropic capital to reduce financial risks and make restoration projects more investable. By using concessional funding from development banks, foundations, or government agencies to absorb early-stage risks, blended finance encourages private sector participation.

- **PPPs** – These partnerships align government funding with private investment to finance large-scale restoration efforts.

- **First-Loss Capital Structures** – Development banks or philanthropic funds take on higher-risk portions of investment, giving private investors greater security.
- **Co-Financing Mechanisms** – Joint funding agreements between multilateral institutions and corporations help scale up restoration finance.

Sustainability-Linked and Green Bonds

New forms of debt instruments, such as SLBs and sovereign green bonds, provide targeted financing for restoration projects:

- SLBs tie financial terms to environmental performance, rewarding issuers with lower interest rates if they meet restoration and conservation goals.
- Green bonds raise capital exclusively for sustainability projects, including reforestation, habitat conservation, and climate adaptation.
- Debt-for-Nature Swaps allow countries to restructure sovereign debt in exchange for commitments to ecosystem restoration.

Market-Based Revenue Models

Integrating restoration finance into established economic markets can create consistent revenue streams:

- **Carbon Markets and Biodiversity Credits** – By monetizing ecosystem services such as carbon sequestration and habitat restoration, projects can generate tradable assets that provide long-term financial returns.
- **PES** – Businesses and municipalities pay for environmental services such as water filtration, soil stabilization, or flood mitigation, creating financial incentives for conservation.
- **Eco-Tourism and Conservation Finance** – Revenue from sustainable tourism, wildlife protection programs, and

conservation-linked businesses can directly fund restoration efforts.

Crowdfunding and Community-Based Investment Models

Engaging individuals, small investors, and local communities in restoration finance can diversify funding sources and increase project ownership.

- **Crowdfunding Platforms** – Online platforms enable the public to contribute directly to restoration initiatives, supporting scalable grassroots funding models.
- **Community Conservation Trusts** – Local investment funds managed by communities ensure that restoration efforts align with long-term sustainability and economic resilience.
- **Microfinance for Restoration** – Small-scale financial instruments provide funding for local landowners and farmers to participate in reforestation and conservation initiatives.

Challenges and Considerations

Despite these new financial models, several challenges remain:

- **Scaling Investment to Meet Global Needs** – While new models are promising, they must be scaled up significantly to meet global restoration targets.
- **Ensuring Transparency and Accountability** – Investors require clear impact measurement frameworks and financial reporting to track restoration progress.
- **Developing Regulatory and Market Stability** – Strengthening legal frameworks for biodiversity credits and ecosystem services can create more predictable investment environments.

Roadmap for Scaling Restoration Finance Globally

Scaling up restoration finance on a global level requires a coordinated approach that aligns financial innovation, policy support, stakeholder engagement, and long-term investment strategies. While progress has been made in mobilizing capital for ecosystem restoration, significant gaps remain in securing sustained funding at the scale required to meet global restoration targets. A clear roadmap is essential to guide public and private actors in expanding financial mechanisms, improving governance, and integrating restoration into mainstream investment frameworks.

Key Steps for Scaling Restoration Finance

1. Strengthening Policy and Regulatory Frameworks

- Governments must establish clear policies, incentives, and legal frameworks to create a stable investment environment for restoration finance.
- Aligning national and international regulations, such as the EU Green Deal, Paris Agreement, and Kunming-Montreal Global Biodiversity Framework, ensures consistency in financing mechanisms.
- Standardizing biodiversity credits and ecosystem service valuation can improve investor confidence and market development.

2. Expanding Blended Finance and De-Risking Mechanisms

- Increasing the use of blended finance models—which combine public, private, and philanthropic capital—reduces financial risks and encourages large-scale investment.
- Governments and development banks can provide first-loss capital, loan guarantees, and co-financing mechanisms to make restoration projects more attractive to private investors.
- Enhancing access to sovereign green bonds and debt-for-nature swaps can help governments allocate financial resources toward large-scale restoration initiatives.

3. Integrating Restoration into Market-Based Solutions

- Strengthening carbon markets, biodiversity credits, and PES creates long-term revenue streams for restoration finance.
- Expanding nature-based solutions in corporate sustainability strategies ensures that businesses contribute financially to restoration efforts.
- Developing sustainability-linked financial instruments, such as sustainability-linked loans and performance-based financing, aligns capital with measurable restoration outcomes.

4. Leveraging Technological and Financial Innovations

- Blockchain and AI-driven monitoring systems improve financial transparency and impact measurement in restoration projects.
- Digital crowdfunding platforms can expand funding opportunities by enabling individuals and small investors to support ecosystem restoration.
- Smart contracts and DeFi models could enhance efficiency in restoration transactions and financial tracking.

5. Strengthening Multi-Stakeholder Partnerships

- Governments, corporations, NGOs, and local communities must collaborate to design, finance, and implement restoration projects at scale.
- PPPs and industry alliances can pool financial resources and technical expertise to support large-scale restoration.

Conclusion

Scaling up sustainable finance for global ecosystem restoration requires a coordinated effort across public and private sectors, financial institutions, and policymakers. While significant progress has been made in mobilizing capital for restoration, achieving the scale necessary to meet global sustainability targets demands innovative financial models, stronger governance frameworks, and expanded investment opportunities. Bridging financial gaps, improving transparency, and fostering collaboration will be essential to unlocking the full potential of restoration finance.

A key challenge in scaling restoration finance is ensuring a steady flow of capital through diversified funding mechanisms. Expanding the use of green bonds, sustainability-linked loans, impact investment funds, and blended finance models can help attract institutional investors while reducing financial risks. Additionally, strengthening carbon and biodiversity markets will create more predictable revenue streams for restoration projects, integrating them into mainstream financial systems.

PPPs and multi-stakeholder collaboration remain critical to achieving large-scale impact. Governments play an essential role in creating enabling policy environments, offering financial incentives, and aligning restoration finance with broader climate and biodiversity commitments. The private sector must continue integrating nature-based solutions into corporate sustainability strategies, ensuring that businesses contribute to restoration efforts while meeting ESG requirements.

Technological innovation, including blockchain for financial transparency, AI-driven impact assessments, and digital crowdfunding platforms, will further support the expansion of restoration finance. These tools enhance accountability, streamline investment processes, and enable broader participation from investors and communities alike. However, regulatory alignment and standardized reporting frameworks are needed to ensure credibility, prevent greenwashing, and build investor confidence.

Despite the challenges, the increasing recognition of ecosystem restoration as a financial and environmental priority presents a significant opportunity for growth. By strengthening financial mechanisms, enhancing governance, and fostering collaboration, restoration finance can transition from a niche investment area to a global economic driver. Ensuring that sustainable finance continues to scale will be essential for achieving long-term environmental resilience and economic sustainability.

Conclusion

Ecosystem restoration is essential for addressing biodiversity loss, climate change, and land degradation, but achieving large-scale impact requires significant financial resources. This book has explored the critical role of sustainable finance in restoration, highlighting a range of financial mechanisms, policy frameworks, and investment strategies that can mobilize capital for long-term ecological recovery.

Public finance and policy incentives remain foundational in de-risking investments and providing structural support for restoration efforts. Market-based mechanisms, such as carbon and biodiversity credits, green bonds, and payments for ecosystem services, offer scalable solutions that align conservation with financial returns. Additionally, impact investment and blended finance models provide opportunities to integrate sustainability objectives into mainstream economic systems.

Technological innovations, including AI, blockchain, and digital crowdfunding, are transforming restoration finance by improving transparency, efficiency, and stakeholder participation. Governance and risk management frameworks ensure financial accountability, enabling restoration projects to attract long-term investment and deliver measurable outcomes.

The Imperative for Financial Sector Involvement

The financial sector has a crucial role in driving the transition toward a sustainable economy by integrating restoration finance into investment portfolios. Institutional investors, asset managers, banks, and corporations must recognize the economic value of ecosystem restoration and actively participate in funding nature-based solutions.

Aligning financial strategies with global sustainability goals presents opportunities for risk mitigation, long-term returns, and enhanced corporate reputation. As regulatory pressures and ESG considerations grow, financial institutions must move beyond corporate sustainability pledges to actively support projects that restore degraded landscapes, protect biodiversity, and enhance climate resilience.

Mainstreaming restoration finance requires the development of standardized investment frameworks, transparent reporting mechanisms, and stronger public-private partnerships. By embedding nature-positive investments into global financial systems, the sector can unlock new capital flows and accelerate large-scale restoration, creating long-term benefits for economies, communities, and ecosystems alike.

Final Call for Action on Policy, Investment, and Innovation

To achieve global restoration goals, financial institutions, policymakers, and investors must take bold action to integrate ecosystem restoration into sustainable finance strategies. Governments must strengthen policy frameworks, offering incentives such as tax benefits, subsidies, and regulatory clarity to attract private sector participation. International financial institutions should expand blended finance initiatives, leveraging public capital to de-risk investments and encourage large-scale funding for restoration projects.

The private sector must move beyond traditional financing approaches by actively supporting market-based mechanisms such as biodiversity credits, sustainability-linked bonds, and impact investment funds. Businesses should incorporate nature-based solutions into corporate sustainability strategies, ensuring that supply chains, operations, and financial portfolios contribute to ecosystem restoration.

Innovation in financial technology will play a key role in increasing transparency, efficiency, and accessibility in restoration finance.

Blockchain, AI-powered monitoring, and digital payment systems must be further integrated to enhance accountability and mobilize new sources of capital.

The path to large-scale ecosystem restoration requires a unified effort across sectors. By prioritizing investment in nature, financial institutions, policymakers, and corporations can drive meaningful change, ensuring that restoration finance transitions from a niche initiative to a core pillar of the global economy. Now is the time to act—scaling up restoration finance will create resilient ecosystems, strengthen economies, and secure a sustainable future for generations to come.

www.ingramcontent.com/pod-product-compliance
Lightning Source LLC
Chambersburg PA
CBHW071604200326
41519CB00021BB/6866